THE
dream
CLEAN

Melbourne-based Chantel Mila, aka Mama Mila, started posting recipes and simple home hacks in 2020, and now has grown a loyal community of over 2.9 million people across platforms. Known for her #mamamilastips series, Chantel creates innovative and well-designed content to her loyal, engaged following. Her relatable style has led her to work with local and global brands including Bunnings, Dyson, Audible, Bed Threads and Adairs. Her media work includes appearances on *The Morning Show*, *Sunrise*, Mamamia, news.com.au and *That's Life* magazine, among many others.

THE
dream
CLEAN

SIMPLE,
BUDGET-FRIENDLY,
ECO-FRIENDLY
WAYS TO MAKE
YOUR HOME
BEAUTIFUL

CHANTEL MILA

SPARKING
IMAGINATION,
CONVERSATION
& CHANGE

First published in 2023 by Pantera Press Pty Limited
www. PanteraPress.com

A Cataloguing-in-Publication entry for this work is available from the National Library of Australia.

ISBN 978-0-6456245-2-6 (Paperback)

Cover and internal design: Elysia Clapin
Front cover photo by Spacejoy on Unsplash
Back cover photo by James Cunningham
Acquiring editor: Tom Langshaw
Proofreader: Marina Sano
Credits for the internal photography can be found at the back of this book
Printed and bound in China by Shenzhen Jinhao Color Printing Co. Ltd.

MIX
Paper from
responsible sources
FSC® C167893

To my kids, Mila and Aston,

who taught me how to appreciate

the small things, and how to remove

the biggest stains

Contents

INTRODUCTION

THE

Dream
Clean

PHILOSOPHY

CHANGE YOUR HABITS, *one day at a time*

When I first moved out of the family home and into my first tiny studio rental, I was 21 years old and was overwhelmed by the number of tasks that went into running a household. I would often wake up to clothes strewn around my bedroom or come home from my full-time job to breakfast dishes in the sink. I'd let it all pile up until the weekend . . . but then, I didn't want to spend all weekend cleaning either.

I started putting aside 15 minutes per day to dedicate towards cleaning my home. As I lived alone at the time, that 15 minutes would be spent doing the dishes, spot-vacuuming, wiping down my bathroom or popping on a load of laundry. I also started my mornings by taking 5 minutes to make my bed, so it was presentable at the day's end.

REDEFINE CLEANING AS *self-care*

These simple and quick habit changes made a big difference to my home and overall mood. The Sunday routine of grocery shopping, opening the windows, deep-cleaning and doing laundry to make the house clean, fresh and organised brought me so much joy. As the months went on, I'd find myself spending my limited paycheques on the latest home-organising items at IKEA over the latest handbag, or I'd purchase a new candle instead of a new lipstick as my form of self-care. That's when I realised: **taking care of my home *was* self-care**.

Against the backdrop of stressful, busy lives, having the ability to clean, organise and style your home can give you an amazing sense of peace. In this book, I'll share with you how to love cleaning – how to stop viewing it as a chore and start viewing it as an empowering habit, a source of pride and joy, a way to deeply take care of yourself by making the environment in which you spend so much of your life a pleasant one.

Go easy ON THE ENVIRONMENT – AND YOUR WALLET

Fast-forward a few years later, to me and my husband living in a 2-bedroom rental with 2 kids under 2 years old. I had much, much less time to clean, but also so many more places that needed to be cleaned. A dilemma I'm sure many new parents will be familiar with! Our unit was very small, and if the place wasn't tidy it felt even smaller. Facing the never-ending piles of laundry and an often overflowing kitchen sink, I started to feel overwhelmed again.

But a new parenting challenge presented me with an opportunity. When my daughter Mila was diagnosed with asthma, I started making my own DIY cleaning products with everyday household items like lemons and bicarb soda. I started safely experimenting with different ingredients and ratios until I found mixes that I absolutely loved. They helped Mila's asthma, were great for the environment, made our home sparkle – and we started seeing significant savings in our tight household budget. **You too can create a beautiful, clean household space without breaking the bank.**

GET THE *whole house* INVOLVED

As my kids got older, we found new ways to get the whole family to take part in keeping the place in order. Mila might have been a toddler, but she loved helping to fold clean laundry and carry the piles to each person's room! My husband and I were juggling work and parenting duties, a juggle that so many households face, so we decided that keeping our home clean and tidy should be a team effort and part of our family time rather than a solo chore at the end of the day. Whether you have a housemate, partner, parents or children living with you, **sharing the workload and mental load of cleaning makes it feel like a place you're all responsible for**.

FIND *joy* IN THE LITTLE THINGS

I've learnt this lesson firsthand from my kids. Sometimes the happiest moments of my day are when I'm doing something completely mundane with them, like folding laundry together while they tell me the smallest details about their day. **Daily care for your home allows you to find joy in everyday moments** that ultimately make up a huge chunk of our lives. There's nothing like the satisfaction of a deep clean, drinking tea in a space you've freshly organised or enjoying the scent of a candle you've lit just for yourself.

MAKE IT *fun*

I always soundtrack my cleaning time. The idea came from my childhood: each Sunday morning, I would wake up to an Enrique Iglesias album playing throughout the house (my mum and aunties were massive Enrique fans!). As soon as we heard 'Hero' playing, we knew it was cleaning time so we'd start pulling the linens off our bed for washing. To this day I still laugh when I hear any of his songs, and it's become an inside family joke. In this book, you'll find plenty of tips and tricks to help make cleaning a household bonding activity, and you'll find playlists before each chapter to help make cleaning fun!

BE *kind* TO YOURSELF

While we can all get caught up in being perfectionists, it's important to keep your expectations realistic. If you have a newborn, a pet and/or a demanding job, it's completely normal for the house to be a mess sometimes. Some days you may only have a few minutes to clean, and that's okay – use that small pocket of time, and celebrate that win. **Try to establish a routine that realistically suits your day-to-day and allows you to do what's important.**

For some people, this will mean simply making sure the sink is tidy every night so that you wake up the next morning to a cleaner space. For others, you might like to soften your linens so you can wake up that little bit more refreshed, or you'll like rolling your towels to make your bathroom feel a bit like a luxury spa. **It's all about making the mundane feel more special**, whatever that means to you.

How to use this book

FLEXIBILITY IS *key*

If you follow me on social media, you might be familiar with some of my viral videos that explain a particular cleaning routine or recipe. I started sharing tips and tricks on social media during Australia's lockdowns with simple, cost-effective ways to turn your home into a place of enjoyment and peace. It's now grown into a wonderful community, and I regularly get asked questions from people all around the world, from different household structures and dynamics.

Here I've brought all of these tips and tricks together into one place, and I've organised these to provide structure to the way you clean. It's designed to be accessible and easy above all. In this book we're going to move through each room of the house, one chapter at a time. Everyone lives in different spaces and cleans in different ways, so feel free to skip ahead to the rooms, furniture and appliances that make most sense for your living situation. Pick and mix among the cleaning checklists. **This is not a one-size-fits-all situation!**

GO WITH THE *flow*

The structure of the book matches the flow of many living spaces. Most modern homes have an open floor plan of a kitchen, dining and living area, so these areas are covered in chapters 1 and 2. Then we move on to the bedroom and bathroom sections, as many homes have ensuites joined to their bedroom – you'll find these areas covered in chapters 3 and 4. Then we move from bathrooms into the laundry in chapter 5, as many homes combine these areas. In many homes the laundry opens out into the outdoor space where you hang your clothes, so the outdoors are covered in chapter 6.

The flow of the book is important in helping you set up your cleaning routines. It's designed to be as accessible, practical and easy as possible, to help you work through the areas of your home in a flow that makes sense for you.

The 3 cleaning routines

As we move through each room, you'll notice there are 3 different levels of routines. These are a general guide on how to structure your cleaning schedule, designed to help you build new habits in your life and build these routines into your day-to-day in a simple but meaningful way. **These checklists are a best-case scenario of what our 'dream clean' looks like.** You won't stay on top of all of these tasks all of the time, and that's okay! **Remember one of our 'dream clean' rules: be kind to yourself.**

These routines are also arranged into checklists – keep this book on your coffee table, in your pantry or on your kitchen benchtop so you have the checklists available when you need them. As every household's cleaning routine will look different, I've also popped a blank template at the end of the book – you can fill it out to create a personalised checklist that works for you. The checklists and routines are broken up into 3 different levels:

Clean in 15: This is your quick-win daily cleaning routine. Remember what I said about how important it is to make cleaning a daily habit? In a quick 15 minutes, you can make sure the mess doesn't build up and become overwhelming. Take the pressure off yourself!

Clean It Like You Mean It: This is for when you have a bit more time to dedicate to cleaning – say, every week or every month. Think of this routine as all those slightly more time-consuming chores or hard-to-reach places that you still need to give some TLC on a semi-regular basis.

Deep Clean: This is your annual spring cleaning routine (or, if you're even more keen, you can do this with every seasonal change). These are all the big-ticket items that involve a bit more elbow grease or moving things around. You'll never feel more at home in your home than after a deep clean – trust me.

HOW-TOs

Within the routines, you'll find an array of how-to guides for cleaning the main spaces within a room alongside the nooks and crannies – commonly used appliances alongside places that everyone forgets to clean. You'll also find plenty of best-practice hacks in breakout boxes, including shortcuts to streamline the cleaning process. And you'll find tricks to get the whole household involved.

DIYs

These are recipes for cleaning products you can make yourself at home, with budget-friendly and accessible ingredients you'll find in most pantries, and you'll also find them under each of the 3 cleaning checklists per room. The DIY sprays, pastes and concoctions are wonderful for the environment, as they're free from harsh chemicals, and are also wonderful for your household budget. These inexpensive, easy-to-follow recipes will transform the way you clean!

Nothing makes me happier than seeing my tips being used, so if you try these DIYs, feel free to tag me on social media: @mama_mila_au and #mamamilastips

ORGANISING

After our deep dive into the 3 cleaning routines, we'll look at how to organise each room, including best-practice tips on home storage. When a space is organised and clutter-free, it's often much easier to keep the area clean. Say goodbye to clutter and say hello to neatly categorised, labelled and stored clusters that can be put out of sight and out of mind. It's important to reduce visual noise around the home to make each room a space that feels calming and pleasant – and allows you and everyone in your family to know that everything has a place. Say goodbye to the days of tripping over mess in the living room or losing your keys somewhere in the kitchen – I'm here to help you.

STYLING

Now that we've made a room clean and hygienic, organised and uncluttered, we'll lastly turn our attention to some inexpensive but fun styling tips that will make your house feel more like a home. It's the small details that can elevate a space into something more cosy and elegant. Remember – cleaning is self-care!

THE *perfect* TRIFECTA

When your home meets the perfect trifecta – clean, organised and styled – that's the Dream Clean. The Dream Clean is a feeling of comfort and warmth. The Dream Clean allows you to make your home a beautiful space. The Dream Clean creates a sanctuary you'll look forward to coming back to at the end of each busy day.

I hope you love this book as much as I've loved creating it!

What you'll need

Making your own DIY sprays means your home will not only look and feel amazing, but you'll also be making a wonderful eco-friendly and budget-friendly switch. There are just a few pantry staples you need to get started.

Spray bottles

I love to use glass spray bottles around the home. They're a great eco-friendly alternative, they keep your DIY sprays fresh and they're easy to label. Start by getting 3–4 bottles, and then buy more as you need them.

Bicarbonate soda

Also known as sodium bicarbonate, bicarbonate of soda, bicarb soda and baking soda, this is an inexpensive way to clean your entire home. It's so versatile – it can be used as a mild abrasive to make cleaning easier, it's a natural deodoriser, a natural clothes brightener and whitener, and it helps break down grime.

> You'll find bicarb soda in the cake-baking aisle of your local supermarket, as it's traditionally used as a raising agent when baking cakes.

White vinegar

While white vinegar might be more familiar to you in the context of cooking or making salad dressings, the acid in the vinegar makes it perfect at breaking down grease, grime and dirt around the house and leaving windows and glass shining. You'll find white vinegar in your grocery store in the sauces and seasonings aisle. Grocery store white vinegar usually has an acidity level of 3–4%. You'll also find cleaning vinegar in the cleaning aisle of your local supermarket – this usually has an acidity level of around 20% and can't be ingested. As a general rule of thumb, white vinegar is great for cleaning inside your home and cleaning vinegar is great for external areas, like windows.

Because of the acidity levels, vinegar is not suitable for some surfaces like porous stone or hardwood floors. Always patch-test before using it around your home.

Tip Never mix vinegar with bleach or chemical cleaners. This combination can create toxic fumes.

Castile soap

This is a versatile vegetable-based soap that's natural, gentle and non-toxic to use around your home. It can be made from coconut, castor, avocado or olive oils, and has wonderful cleaning properties. You can use it as a cleaning product around the home, as well as on your skin.

Dishwashing liquid

This is not just for dishes! Due to its cleansing properties, dishwashing liquid is great at cutting through bathroom stains, removing stains from clothing and cleaning grease from appliances.

Lemons

When life gives you lemons, use them to make your home sparkle! Lemons are an amazing power cleaner. The citric acid within them is amazing at breaking down grease, rust and limescale around the home, leaving areas of the home brightened and smelling fresh.

The power of citric acid: This acid within lemons can be used to remove sweat stains from clothes, make your sink sparkle, remove limescale from your kettle, brighten clothes, clean your chopping boards . . . the uses are endless.

Essential oils

While we all know that essential oils are wonderful at adding natural fragrance to your home, they also have many wonderful cleaning benefits. These are my top 5 essential oil recommendations for beginners:

◊ **Clove oil** – has antibacterial and antifungal properties, and is great to combat mould spores around the home.

◊ **Tea-tree oil** – also has antibacterial and antifungal properties, and is great to use in bathroom sprays and to help with stain removal.

◊ **Lavender oil** – a wonderful antibacterial and deodoriser that also has a calming and peaceful smell. It helps repel dustmites, so it's wonderful in room and linen sprays.

◊ **Lemon oil** – has antibacterial agents and helps leave areas of the home with a natural shine. Due to its fresh fragrance, it's great to use around the kitchen.

◊ **Eucalyptus oil** – a natural antibacterial with disinfectant pro-perties. It's wonderful to use around the bathroom and in the washing machine for stain removal.

Tip

Some essential oils may not be suitable for households with pets or young children. Check the bottle for disclaimers before use.

Another way to gently add natural fragrance to your DIY sprays is to use a small amount of vanilla extract.

Throughout this book you'll also find some less traditional methods of cleaning.

Denture tablets

Did you know that denture tablets have whitening and effervescent properties that not only work for dentures, but also for whitening clothes, toilets, sinks and drink bottles?

Shaving cream

This is wonderful at removing tough spills like red wine stains due to its foamy texture. When you buff shaving cream with a microfibre cloth across glass surfaces in the home – like external oven glass or bathroom cabinets – it leaves an invisible layer which shines, keeps fingerprints away for longer and prevents glass from fogging. A little goes a very long way, so only use sparingly.

Here's a shopping list to get you started:

HOME ESSENTIALS CHECKLIST

☐ 3–4 glass spray bottles

☐ 1 kg box bicarb soda

☐ 2L white vinegar

☐ 1 bottle castile soap

☐ 1 bottle dishwashing liquid

☐ 2–3 lemons

☐ 5 essential oils

INGREDIENTS

CLEVER TOOLS TO MAKE CLEANING EASIER

There are so many tools and gadgets that are designed to make cleaning a little easier. Investing in the right tools could mean hours being saved down the track, so choose the ones that work best for your space and enjoy the extra time saved!

Microfibre mops
These come with multiple mop heads, so they can be used to dry dust around the whole home, and when damp, they're wonderful to use on hardwood or timber floors. You can also use them to clean walls and baseboards with ease.

Microfibre or bamboo cloths
As the name suggests, these are made from very small fibres woven together. This construction makes cleaning easier as dirt, dust and bacteria are captured by the cloth. Microfibre cloths are also very absorbent and dry quickly. You can launder them within your washing machine frequently so you always have a fresh cloth to use. They're perfect for the areas where you need to be a little more gentle, like shower screens, glass, benchtops, porcelain vanities and mirrors. Say goodbye to overused paper towels and sponges!

Another great alternative to microfibre cloths are bamboo cloths, which are made purely from bamboo and are biodegradable.

Power scrubbers
These small, cordless machines help you scrub tough areas around the home, a simple investment to make cleaning easier. There are power cleaners that help with small but tough-to-clean areas – like around your stovetop – and some that are large and telescopic to help with larger areas of the home, like decking or grout. They often come in different sizes, with differently shaped heads for different surfaces. Some come with poles and extensions for harder-to-reach areas.

Non-abrasive scrubbing pads

These pads are made from a tough material that can help cut through tough grime without scratching the surface. They're a great tool for removing limescale from showers and rings from bathtubs, for example.

Cleaning toothbrushes

This is an old trick of course, but you can use any old toothbrush to clean tight nooks and crannies within your home, including shower railings, windowsills, shower door bases, taps, faucets and sink overflows.

Grout brush

These are stiff, thin brushes that can be used to clean tight corners of your bathroom, for example on grout, with a bit more force.

HOME ESSENTIALS CHECKLIST

☐ Vacuum cleaner

☐ Broom

☐ Mop

☐ Bucket

☐ 3–4 microfibre cloths

EQUIPMENT

CHAPTER 1

The kitchen is truly the heart of the home. In our household, it's where we start and end our busy days together as a family, the place where we hear about all the schoolyard updates. Even when I was growing up, our dining room table was where secrets were shared, the funniest family jokes were told, where we gathered for celebrations and milestones, and where the biggest bonding moments took place.

The flipside of a place that is used so frequently is that it can feel overwhelming to keep clean and in control of. **A simple rule: the easiest way to keep a tidy kitchen is to tidy up after every use.** As my mum used to say, 'If you do it now, it will take you seconds; if you do it later, it will take you hours.' It's one of those mantras that has always been in the back of my mind.

Sometimes, at the end of a busy day, cleaning the kitchen will feel like the last thing you want to do. But taking those 10–15 minutes to do a quick kitchen clean can make a big difference the next morning. **Is there any better way to start your day than walking into a fresh kitchen?** It makes the morning rush just a bit smoother, allowing you to feel more organised and refreshed. That clear mindset is a powerful asset to start your day with.

As the kitchen is shared by all members of the household, **it's a great area to get the whole family involved in.** This could be in a rotating roster, or just assigning small tasks to each member at the end of the day. Even younger kids can get involved in the kitchen cleaning routine: my kids love helping to empty the dishwasher and categorise cutlery in its correct spot. And if you get more people to help out in the evenings, that 15 minutes could be cut down to 5 minutes – many hands do make light work.

Every household is different, and depending on work and lifestyle, what is achievable for one household may not work for another. When you have a very busy week and need a 'quick win' clean, the Clean in 15 is for you. When you have a bit more time, or have more members of the household to help you, you can try to fit in Deep Clean items.

Make kitchen cleaning part of your daily self-care. Put on your favourite playlist, get the family involved and incorporate those few minutes into your nightly routine. Allow yourself to start your mornings fresh!

CLEANING *playlist*

As I've mentioned, music makes the cleaning process feel much quicker and more enjoyable for me. I've compiled a playlist on Spotify with some of my favourite songs, and at the beginning of each chapter you'll find the code below to take you to the music. Simply open your Spotify app, click Search, click on the camera icon in the top right corner, and point your phone's camera at the Spotify code printed below. Happy listening!

Clean in 15

A nightly kitchen reset can be the simplest way to keep your home feeling fresh and manageable. Start by loading your plates into your dishwasher, give your sink a quick clean, clear any benchtop clutter and wipe down your benchtops and splashback. This simple routine only takes around 15 minutes to do, but it makes such a difference.

CHECKLIST

☐ Load dishwasher

☐ Hand-wash any larger dishes (e.g. pots and pans)

☐ Clean sink

☐ Clear and wipe benchtops

☐ Wipe stovetop

☐ Wipe splashback

☐ Wash microfibre cloths

☐ Spot-vacuum

☐ Pack away stray items

☐ Take out bins

For the dining / meals area:

☐ Clear dishes

☐ Wipe down table and chairs

☐ Vacuum chair upholstery

☐ Vacuum around and under table

DIY Multipurpose Spray

If you need one spray that can do it all, this is the one for you! This DIY multipurpose spray can be used throughout the entire house, and you'll see it mentioned a few times in the book. It's so versatile – the acidity from the white vinegar helps make cleaning quick and easy.

You'll need:

- 1 cup water
- ½ cup white vinegar
- 20 drops essential oil of your choice (depending on preferred fragrance)
- Spray bottle

How to:

- Mix water, vinegar and essential oil in spray bottle.
- Shake to combine. It's as easy as that!

White vinegar is a mild acid and may not be suitable for all surfaces around the home, especially porous surfaces like marble or natural stone.

Here's an alternative method you can use:

- 1 cup water
- 2 tsp castile soap
- 10 drops essential oil of your choice

DIY Multipurpose Spray with Lemons

This spray uses a wonderful mix of white vinegar and the citric acid within the lemons for a powerful way to remove spills, mess and grime.

You'll need:

- 1 cup white vinegar
- 1 lemon (or lemon peels)
- 2 sprigs rosemary
- Jar with a lid
- Strainer
- Spray bottle
- 1 cup water

How to:

- Mix white vinegar, lemon and rosemary in an airtight jar.
- Infuse for 7–14 days for a strong citrus scent.
- Strain into a spray bottle.
- Dilute with water.

Tip When you finish using a lemon or lime, sprinkle baking soda over the segment and rub it on your sink. An easy way to keep your sink smelling great and looking shiny!

HOW TO CLEAN YOUR SINK

A lot of food waste and dirty dishes pass through your sink, so it can be a hotspot where bacteria lurk. Cleaning it on a daily basis helps protect you and your family from those nasties, keeping you healthy and safe.

You'll need:

- ¼ cup baking soda
- 1 tbsp dishwashing liquid
- Microfibre cloth

How to:

- Sprinkle baking soda over sink.
- Pour dishwashing liquid on top of baking soda.
- Buff mixture in with a damp microfibre cloth until clean, then rinse with water.

After using this method, you can buff baby oil into your sink with a microfibre cloth to keep it shiny for longer.

HOW TO REMOVE SPOT STAINS FROM UPHOLSTERY CHAIRS

If you have upholstery chairs at your dining table, spot stains and spills are inevitable, especially if you have kids. But there are simple ways to refresh your fabric furniture!

For spot stains:
In a spray bottle, mix ½ cup soda water with 2 tsp dishwashing liquid. This can also be used daily or weekly to keep minor stains away.

For a deeper clean:
Look up portable upholstery and carpet spot cleaners. These are small machines that deep clean your upholstery and also remove the excess water, so there's no staining left under the fabric. You can purchase one, or many places have them for short-term hire as well.

HOW TO REDUCE YOUR MENTAL LOAD

Managing a household with these daily Clean in 15 routines can be a daunting challenge. 'Mental load' is a term I first heard of when my son, Aston, was a newborn, and it changed my life. I couldn't understand why I had been so mentally exhausted at the end of each day, and now I knew: it was from constantly having to plan for and organise the household.

The mental load is the running checklist at the back of your mind. It's all the invisible labour you put into running a household – for example, knowing the due dates of bills, when the kids finish school early, menu planning, grocery shopping, doctors appointments, play dates, clothes rotations, excursions, parties and work deadlines.

The good news is, there's a way to ease your mental load, and it means getting the whole family or household involved! Here are some simple steps to ensure you're taking care of yourself while also keeping on top of these daily tasks:

◊ **Talk about it:** Speak to the other members of your household and explain how you're feeling. Look at simple ways you can share some of the workload together. Starting the conversation is the best way to reframe how you manage household tasks.

◊ **Routines and rosters:** Once your household is aware of the items that take up the mental load, it's time to share them around. This could be as simple as giving your partner the responsibility to look after all bills and payments and all grocery shopping and meal planning. Taking one or two large items off your plate is a great place to start.

◊ **Shared calendars:** This one has been a game-changer in our household! We created a household email address and then linked our phone calendars to that shared email address. Anything put into the calendar appeared on everyone's phones at the same time, so we could allocate tasks and all be aware of upcoming events. This doesn't need to be digital; a simple calendar in a communal area (for example, the kitchen fridge) is also a great way to share key dates.

◊ **After-Dinner Time (ADT):** Get the whole family involved in a 15-minute clean after dinner – this is your 'ADT'. Play some music, or use the time to catch up with each other as you wash dishes, clean benchtops and tidy up the kitchen table. Make it a part of your daily household routine so it's not a standalone chore but something you all do together.

Clean it *like you mean it*

The tasks in this section are perfect for a Sunday morning reset, when you may have the time to do a more thorough clean of your kitchen. It's easy to incorporate some of these into your weekly routine – for example, you can check your pantry and fridge for items close to expiry before doing your weekly grocery shop. The more you incorporate these throughout the week, the less time they'll take and the less intimidating the idea of cleaning will become.

CHECKLIST

☐ Check pantry for expired items and wipe down with multipurpose spray

☐ Check fridge and freezer for expired items and wipe down with fridge spray

☐ Clean microwave

☐ Clean stovetop

☐ Mop floors

☐ Clean splashbacks

☐ Move small appliances and wipe underneath them

☐ Wipe down light switches, powerpoints and doorknobs

☐ Wash tea towels

☐ Replace sponges and sponge head on your dish brush

☐ Wash bin and bin area

☐ Wash walls behind pet bowls

WEEKLY / MONTHLY KITCHEN CLEAN

DIY Fridge Spray

You'll need:

- Spray bottle
- 1 cup warm water
- ¼ cup white vinegar
- 2 tbsp vanilla extract
- Microfibre cloth

Vanilla extract makes this DIY spray smell amazing. For a different scent, you can swap it out for 2–3 drops of your favourite essential oil.

How to:

- In a spray bottle mix water, vinegar and vanilla extract.
- Simply spray in your fridge and wipe with a damp microfibre cloth!

HOW TO CLEAN A FRIDGE

Did you know that cleaning your fridge can help you save money? Before completing your weekly grocery shop, dedicate 15 minutes to your fridge. Clear out any expired items, look at what's about to expire and plan your grocery shop around those items. (See also my tips on how to organise your fridge later in this chapter!)

This way you can avoid wastage, keep on top of expiry dates and save money by avoiding the accidental purchase of duplicate items. While you're doing your 15-minute clear-out, you can use this DIY fridge spray to wipe up any spills that have occurred to keep it fresh and clean. When you return from your grocery shop, you'll be restocking into a clean and fresh fridge.

Tip Place a small bowl of baking soda or used coffee grounds in the fridge to keep your fridge deodorised for longer.

HOW TO CLEAN A MICROWAVE

Everyone uses their microwave a different amount; I know of some households that rely heavily on their microwave, while others don't even own one. If you use yours frequently, you may notice that food splatters can dry on the sides and harden, making them very difficult to clean.

The great news is that there is a quick and easy way to remove the mess without the need for heavy scrubbing. This method creates a steam environment that softens all the stubborn, baked-on food, making it easy to clean. Doing this every couple of weeks, or whenever you have tough food mess to remove, will keep your microwave clean and sparkling.

You'll need:

- 1 cup water
- 1 tsp dishwashing liquid (this can be substituted for 2 tbsp white vinegar or 2 slices lemon)
- Deep microwave-safe bowl

How to:

- Mix water and dishwashing liquid in bowl.
- Place in microwave and heat for 4 minutes. (Note: Every microwave has a different wattage, so your timing may need to be adjusted accordingly.)
- Allow bowl to sit in microwave for another 4 minutes before opening door.
- Carefully remove bowl with oven mitts.
- There should be condensation all through the inside of the microwave. Gently wipe and watch the grime slide off.

A word of caution for this method: never leave the microwave unattended, and don't let the mixture bubble over!

HOW TO CLEAN A GAS STOVETOP

Our stovetops are where cooking magic happens, but they can also be where the biggest messes are made. The DIY multipurpose spray is great at removing daily spills from this area, but sometimes you need a deep clean to remove burnt or cooked-on mess.

This method works best when applied weekly to your stovetop. The dishwashing liquid and white vinegar work together to help break down grease, and the baking soda makes it easier to clear away.

You'll need:

- 2 tbsp dishwashing liquid
- ½ cup baking soda
- 1 tbsp water
- Spray bottle filled with white vinegar
- Microfibre cloth

How to:

- Fill sink with hot water and 1 tbsp dishwashing liquid. Remove stovetop grates and soak them.
- Mix baking soda and 1 tbsp dishwashing liquid with enough water to form a paste.
- Apply paste to only external areas of stovetops and burners – ensure it does not touch any internal areas.
- Leave for 30 minutes.
- Spray a small amount of white vinegar over mix.
- Wipe with microfibre cloth to reveal your clean stovetop.
- Wash and replace stovetop grates.

There are tools available to make cleaning tricky areas like stovetops easier. Look up 'handheld power scrubbers' to save you a lot of time!

HOW TO CLEAN AN INDUCTION STOVETOP

Because induction stovetops are made of glass, the cleaning process is a bit more delicate. A spray of white vinegar wiped down with a microfibre cloth should help remove day-to-day spills, but this DIY is perfect if you need something more powerful to cut through cloudiness or tough stains.

You'll need:

- Baking soda
- 1 lemon
- Microfibre cloth

How to:

- Sprinkle a thin layer of baking soda across your induction stovetop.
- Cut a lemon in half and remove the pips.
- Rub the inside of the halved lemon against the stovetop in gentle circular motions, making sure to not scratch your stovetop.
- Wipe away the mixture with a microfibre cloth.

DIY Floor Cleaner

Kitchen floors can hold so much hidden dirt and grime. Think about how much they're used in an average week – in our home, floors have mud, sand, dirt, dust and allergens tracked through them daily (and that's just by my 4-year-old!). It's good to give them some TLC at least once a week.

You'll need:

- 2 cups warm water
- ½ cup white vinegar
- ½ tsp dishwashing liquid
- ¼ cup isopropyl (rubbing) alcohol (optional)
- 10 drops essential oil of your choice
- Mop

Not all essential oils are suitable around babies and pets. You can leave out the essential oils for a fragrance-free option.

How to:

- Mix together in a bucket the water, white vinegar, dishwashing liquid, isopropyl alcohol and essential oil.
- Mop your floors with this mixture to leave them sparkling clean.

Vinegar is a mild acid and not suitable for some floor types like marble or hardwood. If you need a more gentle cleaner, try this mix instead:

- 2 cups warm water
- 2 tsp castile soap
- 4 drops essential oil of your choice (optional)

HOW TO CLEAN A GLASS SPLASHBACK

When we cook, grease and oil can splatter everywhere. This simple mix cuts through greasy mess and leaves your glass splashback looking clean and streak-free. You can use this mix, or the DIY multipurpose spray (see page 31), to leave your splashbacks shining.

You'll need:

- Spray bottle
- 2 cups warm water
- 1 cup white vinegar
- 6 drops lemon essential oil or lemon juice
- Microfibre cloth

How to:

- Mix all ingredients in a spray bottle.
- Shake to combine, then spray and wipe surfaces with a microfibre cloth. This simple mix cuts through grease and leaves glass splashbacks shining!

HOW TO CLEAN A MARBLE OR STONE SPLASHBACK

These materials look beautiful, but they also require a little bit more care due to the finish. The castile soap in this method is a great alternative to vinegar that will leave these surfaces sparkling.

You'll need:

- Spray bottle
- 2 cups warm water
- 2 tsp castile soap
- 4 drops essential oil of your choice (optional)
- Microfibre cloth

Tip This gentle cleaner is suitable for most surfaces around the home that require gentle care, such as stone benchtops.

How to:

- In a spray bottle, mix water, castile soap and essential oil.
- Shake to combine, then spray and wipe surfaces.

PLACES EVERYONE FORGETS
TO CLEAN IN THE KITCHEN (PART 1)

Underneath appliances
Disconnect all small appliances, like kettles, toasters and microwaves, and wipe underneath them. You'll be amazed at what you find under there! This should be done monthly.

Light switches, powerpoints and doorknobs
Especially if you've had any viruses within your home, these high-touch areas can become breeding grounds for germs and bacteria. Simply wiping them using a multipurpose spray once a week will help keep those germs away.

Garbage bins and the area they're kept in
Each time you take out the bin, make it part of your routine to give your bin area a quick wipe down with a multipurpose spray. Every 2 weeks, give the whole garbage bin a complete rinse and clean to remove any food debris and scraps that may have spilt on it.

The wall behind pet food bowls
This area can accumulate a lot of spills and splashes. Give it a quick wipe down about once a week.

Deep *clean*

You know those mornings when you wake up and feel the mood to deep-clean and rearrange your entire home? This section of the book is for those mornings! These tasks only need to be done at monthly, seasonal or even annual intervals – and can be allocated to different family members to get the whole household involved – but they make a big difference to the feeling of your home. The frequency you do these cleans is completely up to you and what works for your household.

CHECKLIST

KITCHEN DEEP CLEAN

☐ Clean kettle

☐ Clean toaster

☐ Descale coffee machine

☐ Clean kitchen cabinets

☐ Clean oven

☐ Clean oven warming drawer

☐ Clean rangehood

☐ Clean dishwasher

☐ Clear out and rinse drawer dividers and organisers

☐ Wipe inside cabinets

☐ Vacuum fridge coils

☐ Wipe light fixtures

HOW TO CLEAN A KETTLE

When was the last time you looked inside your kettle? Unless you've cleaned it recently, it's likely to have black limescale build-up. The great news is that the limescale is very quick and easy to clean. This method should be applied every month on average, but you can base the frequency on how often you use your kettle.

You'll need:
- Water
- 1 sliced lemon

How to:
- Fill kettle with water and add lemon.
- Boil twice.
- Allow to stand for 15–30 minutes.
- Empty and rinse kettle with tap water.

HOW TO CLEAN A TOASTER

Toasters can be one of the trickiest items to clean, as crumbs can get caught in so many tight crevices. If your love of avocado toast is as strong as mine is, your toaster may be on high rotation. Due to its heavy use, monthly cleaning is a must to avoid fire hazards from crumbs burning inside the toaster.

You'll need:
- Hairdryer
- ¼ cup water
- ¼ cup white vinegar
- Microfibre cloth

How to:
- Unplug your toaster.
- Use a hairdryer on the lowest setting to gently dislodge any stuck crumbs down to the bottom of the machine.
- Remove your toaster trays at the bottom of the machine and wipe them. Make sure they're dry before returning them.
- To clean the outside of the toaster, mix water and white vinegar in a spray bottle and wipe clean.

DIY Kitchen Cabinet Cleaner

Kitchen cabinets attract oily and sticky fingerprint marks. Depending on the type of finish on your cabinets, keeping them fingerprint-free can be a nearly impossible task. A nightly wipe with a multipurpose spray could be all you need to keep fingerprints and grease splatters away – but if you need a heavy-duty, deep clean, this DIY is for you. Doing it every quarter will keep your kitchen cabinets shining. Remember to always patch-test, as every kitchen cabinet finish is different.

You'll need:

- ½ cup baking soda
- 1 tsp lemon juice
- 1 cup warm water
- Microfibre cloth

How to:

- Mix the baking soda, lemon juice and water together to make a liquidy paste.
- Apply the paste on your cabinets with a microfibre cloth.
- Leave for 2–3 minutes.
- Wipe off with warm water and a clean microfibre cloth.

Tip

You can use either fresh or bottled lemon juice for this DIY.

WHY DO WE SPRING CLEAN?

Spring-cleaning season is a chance to do a large cleanout of our entire home. After long winters in which we've spent a lot of time at home with heaters on, we look to remove dust and allergens before the onset of allergy season. It's also a great time to declutter by throwing out unneeded items from your home, in order to decrease visual noise and in turn reduce your stress levels! The lead-up to the new year is another great time to get your home clean and in order, to start afresh.

HOW TO CLEAN AN OVEN

Traditional oven cleaners often have strong fumes that can be uncomfortable to breathe in. This lower-tox alternative is not completely scrub-free, but it does help to break down baked-on grease and make the process much easier. On average, this process can be applied once a quarter, or when needed. Before following this process, check your oven manual for the best cleaning method, as they're all different.

You'll need:

- ½ cup baking soda
- 1 tbsp dishwashing liquid
- 2 tbsp water
- Microfibre cloth
- Spray bottle with white vinegar

How to:

- Mix together baking soda, dishwashing liquid and water to make a smooth paste.
- Apply a thin layer of the paste to the inside of the oven, avoiding vents and openings, and leave overnight.
- The next day, wipe down oven and scrub any difficult areas, then spray with white vinegar to help remove any residue.

HOW TO CLEAN A DISHWASHER

This is a simple process to deep-clean your dishwasher. It's important to do this fairly regularly in order to keep the appliance running efficiently – to keep your plates shining – and to make sure the machine is in good working order longer-term. Note: before following this process, check your manual first to see the best way to deep-clean your dishwasher.

You'll need:

- 1 cup white vinegar
- Dishwasher-safe cup

How to:

- Remove the dishwasher filter (check your manual to see how to remove your model's filter).
- Empty, soak, wash and return filter.
- Fill 1 cup with white vinegar and place on the top shelf of your dishwasher.
- Run the machine empty on the hottest setting. The white vinegar helps to clean and deodorise the dishwasher.
- Leave the machine door open and allow it to air-dry before using it again.

HOW TO CLEAN RANGEHOOD FILTERS

These can attract a lot of oil and debris, so it's important to keep them clean and deodorised. Although rangehood filters can look daunting, they are surprisingly easy to clean! Note: before following this process, check your manual first to see the best way to clean your rangehood filters.

You'll need:
- 1 tsp dishwashing liquid
- 1 cup baking soda
- Bristled brush

How to:
- Soak filters in very hot water and add a squeeze of dishwashing liquid.
- Rotate them after 5 minutes so both sides are soaked.
- Sprinkle 1 cup of baking soda and wipe with a bristled brush. This helps to remove any crumbs or tougher stains.
- Place the filters in the dishwasher and allow to air-dry.

Tip In between deep cleans, you can run your filters through the dishwasher regularly to keep them maintained. Check your manual to ensure your rangehood filters are dishwasher-safe.

PLACES EVERYONE FORGETS TO CLEAN IN THE KITCHEN (PART 2)

Refrigerator coils

These are located at the back of the fridge and should be cleaned once a year. If you're finding your fridge isn't as cold as it once was, it could be due to build-up on the coils. To clean them, disconnect the fridge from the power and locate the coils. (Check your manual – they're usually at the back.) Vacuum the coils with a small crevice attachment to remove all the dust, then plug your fridge back in ready to use again.

Light fixtures

These can build up a lot of dust. Giving them a quick wipe down every 3–4 months will not only remove the dust but also make your house look brighter.

The warming drawer of the oven

You know that little drawer underneath your oven? It's actually for warming food once you've taken it out from the oven. Whether you use it or not, give it a wipe down each time you clean your oven, as food and debris can fall into this area.

KITCHEN CLEANING *tips and tricks*

How to remove rust from knives

Even the best knives can develop rust spots from time to time due to oxidisation. Proper care, like not placing knives into the dishwasher, can help prevent rust. If you do find yourself with rust spots, the great news is that they're very easy to remove.

- ◊ Sprinkle the rust-affected area with baking soda.
- ◊ Squeeze lemon juice on top of the baking soda.
- ◊ The mixture will fizz. Leave for 15 minutes.
- ◊ Gently buff away the mixture and the rust will be gone!

How to make cutlery and glassware shine

Cutlery can be tarnished when the silver is exposed to oxygen, usually after being placed in the dishwasher. Wineglasses and other glasses can also become foggy. But making silverware and glassware shine again is easy!

- ◊ Mix 1 part vinegar to 4 parts water in a bowl.
- ◊ Add your cutlery or glassware and allow to soak for 15 minutes.
- ◊ Rinse and dry using a lint-free cloth.

How to make dishes dry faster

Once you finish running your dishwasher, drape a dry tea towel over the top of the door and close the dishwasher again. The tea towel helps absorb excess moisture to allow the dishes to dry faster. And if your dishwasher has a space for rinse aid, always make sure this is topped up.

HOW TO CLEAN TRICKY UTENSILS

How to clean your cheese grater
If your grater has bits of cheese stuck inside it, a quick way to clean those tricky and sharp holes is to grate some raw potato! This helps push out the stuck food.

How to clean your wooden spoons
These can attract a lot of oil that goes rancid inside the spoon. One handy hack, which has been previously endorsed by celebrity chef Matt Preston, is to place your wooden spoon in boiling water – this draws all the oil out from the spoon and into the hot water. Leave for about 10 minutes, then rinse and coat with fresh oil to keep the wood protected.

How to clean wooden chopping boards
A simple way to clean these is with salt and a lemon – simply sprinkle salt over your wooden chopping board and rub half a lemon over the top. This helps remove stubborn stains and leaves the boards fresh and deodorised. After, coat with wood oil to keep the wood protected.

How to clean stainless steel appliances
Baby oil is wonderful at making stainless steel appliances shine. Simply apply a small amount to a microfibre cloth and buff in the direction of the stainless steel to keep it shiny and fingerprint-free. In our household, this hack was a game-changer for removing little fingerprint marks on the fridge!

Organising

A well-organised kitchen can help you keep your kitchen cleaner. Organisation is a large part of keeping your home feeling clean and tidy – because when everything has a place to be stored, it prevents clutter and allows high-use areas to run more smoothly.

The first step to organising any space around the home is to declutter and donate any items you no longer use. Some great places to start are your cup drawer, your cutlery drawer and your storage containers. Often we've unconsciously decided that some items are our go-tos, like our favourite coffee mugs, while we never use others.

When you have an hour on a quiet afternoon, empty some drawers and cabinets in your kitchen and have a look at what you need and what you don't. Return only the items you use or those that have sentimental value, and donate the rest.

HOW TO ORGANISE YOUR FRIDGE

◊ Measure your fridge's shelves and internal compartments to find the best sized boxes and storage solutions that will work for your space.

◊ Look at the food you regularly buy, and group items by categories. Common categories are meats, yoghurt, cheese, vegetables, fruit, salads, condiments and drinks.

◊ Purchase storage boxes and containers that fit your fridge and fit your categories, or find containers from around your home that are fridge-safe.

Tip Opt for clear storage containers so you can see items in your fridge easily.

Tip Utilise turntables inside your fridge to make reaching condiments easier, so you don't end up with some stuck at the back.

The door is the warmest part of your fridge (perfect for condiments) and the bottom shelf is the coldest part of your fridge (perfect for meat or vegetables).

FOOD STORAGE TIPS FOR *fridge and pantry*

◊ **Berries:** Soak in ¾ cup water and ¼ cup white vinegar for 10 minutes, then rinse well and dry. Store in an airtight container lined with paper towels.

◊ **Greens:** Store wrapped in a damp paper towel in an airtight container.

◊ **Carrots and celery:** Store with the bottom soaking in a glass jar to keep them crunchy for longer.

◊ **Lemons:** If you only need a small amount of lemon juice from your lemon, roll it on your countertop and poke a hole with a skewer at the top. You can squeeze the lemon to use the juice without the rest of it drying out!

◊ **Avocados:** Keep them from browning with a few drops of lemon juice on the inside.

◊ **Herbs:** Store in a bouquet with water to keep them fresher. You can place a ziplock bag over the top of the bouquet too.

◊ **Tomatoes:** Store upside down to increase their shelf life.

◊ **Nut butter:** Store upside down to prevent separation.

◊ **Brown sugar:** Place a marshmallow in your brown sugar to avoid it going hard.

As in the fridge, keep items that you commonly use in your pantry on a turntable for easy and quick access. This could be items like oil, salt, pepper, sauces and seasonings. You can also keep this turntable in a cabinet near your stovetop so it's easily accessible when cooking.

Tip Don't forget the power of your freezer to preserve food for longer! Items like tomato puree can be frozen in ice cube trays and can be used in individual servings later on. Items like wilted spinach and bananas can be frozen for smoothies.

STORAGE TIPS FOR YOUR *spice rack*

Your spice rack can consist of many different-shaped containers and packets, which looks messy! Here are some simple tips to make organising this space easier:

1. Empty your spice collection by clearing out any expired items.
2. Look at which spices you have in your kitchen, how often you use them and the size of the packets you purchase.
3. If your spices are in packets, source glass jars to store them in, in the size and quantity you require.

Tip Depending on your cupboard arrangement, you can store your spices on a rotating turntable or on tiered shelving for easier access.

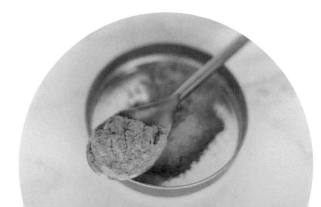

STORAGE TIPS FOR *small appliances*

As a rule of thumb, it's best to leave benchtops clear and clutter-free. This helps reduce visual noise, allows for more space to prepare meals and helps us stay more organised. With the exception of a few items, I like to keep small appliances within the cupboards and keep my benchtops clear.

A quick way to decide which items should be stored within your cupboards and which ones should go on your benchtops is to look at your daily use of them:

1. Do I use this appliance every day?
2. Is it difficult to move?
3. Is it difficult to fit in my cupboards?

If the answer is yes to all three questions, then it's best to keep it on your benchtop. If no, then your cupboard may be the best spot.

Some people like to have their knife blocks on display as they are frequently used items, but others believe it's very bad feng shui – this is a personal choice!

Tip To keep small appliance wires from tangling in storage, you can place 2 stick-on hooks on the back of the appliance and use the hooks to wrap the wires neatly around the appliance.

STORAGE TIPS FOR *Tupperware*

The trick to keeping Tupperware organised to maximise storage space is to keep the boxes and lids separate. Stack boxes from largest to smallest on one side of your cupboard, and on the other side, stack lids vertically in a small office organiser.

STORAGE TIPS FOR *around the sink*

This area can be prone to clutter, including drying dishes, sprays, dish brushes, gloves and sponges. A simple way to clear it, without having to move these items away from their convenient places, is with a small tray. This helps to reduce clutter and categorises the items into clusters.

STORAGE TIPS FOR *under the sink*

This area can collect so many sprays and bottles, and is often trickier to organise because of all the under-sink plumbing. There are a few tricks to maximise storage space:

- ◊ Running a tension rod across your under-sink area is a quick way to increase space and allows for a place to hang spray bottles.

- ◊ Stackable office drawers can be used to store microfibre cloths, sponge heads, gloves and bin bags.

- ◊ Wire baskets are great for this space as they are easy to see through but also can be easily cleaned.

- ◊ Adding stick-on hooks to your cupboard doors can provide a great space to hang your microfibre cloths and tea towels.

Tip As this space can be a wet zone, labelled containers are great to store items you don't want getting wet (like tea towels or cloths).

See **chapter 5** for the best way to wash microfibre cloths!

HOW TO ORGANISE KITCHEN CUPBOARDS

The easiest way to keep your kitchen cabinets tidy all year round is to have a great storage system that makes it easy to stay organised. We use plates, bowls, cutlery and glasses every day, so keeping them easily accessible at waist height is important. Then the less frequently used items like fine china, collectors glasses or party items are stored in higher or harder-to-reach areas of the kitchen.

These simple tips can help make organising easy:

◊ Use an office file rack to vertically store baking trays, roasting pans and chopping boards.

◊ Smaller office file racks are perfect for organising Tupperware lids.

◊ Use wine racks to store drink bottles. This will help you grab your favourite drink bottle easily without them all falling over.

◊ Place a chopping board on top of your sink when it's not in use – a simple way to increase bench space within your kitchen!

◊ Attach magazine holders to the internal side of your cupboards for storing baking paper and cling wraps.

◊ If you have deep cupboards, items can often get lost at the back. A simple solution is to use tiered shelving, so the items at the back are taller than those at the front.

◊ Another solution for deep cupboards is to add turntables so that items can be rotated to find the one you're looking for easily.

Styling

Since we spend a lot of time in our kitchen, it's important to make it a place you feel comfortable and relaxed in. It's also prone to clutter, so I find a 'less is more' approach helps when styling this area of the home. To style your benchtops, you could use a mini grouping of a plant, book or candle and leave the rest of your benchtops clear. Or you could bring in the items you use most frequently into your styling, like hanging your favourite mugs near your coffee machine, or investing in a great fruit bowl to display your fruit. Keep it simple!

QUICK *kitchen styling* TIPS

How to manage paper clutter
This can take up a lot of room on our benchtops – think bills, homework or receipts. A simple solution is using office dividers to vertically store kitchen paperwork so it's categorised and off the benchtop.

Make mini vignettes: 3–4 styling items
Vignettes are a grouping of décor items, and these work really well in the kitchen to brighten up corners. Lay a wooden chopping board vertical against your splashback (you can also cover any powerpoints) and style 2–4 items at the front such as flowers, a candle, cookbooks, and/or your mortar and pestle.

Use shelving to create more space
You can use mini shelving to create more benchtop space.

Look at your 'top dumped' items
Look at which items end up taking up space on your benchtops and find 'homes' for those items. In our home, my husband loves to empty his pockets and leave his keys and loose change on the benchtops, so we repurposed a small used candle jar which is now the 'home' for those items on our benchtop.

Kitchen routines and checklists

CHECKLIST

DAILY KITCHEN CLEAN

- ☐ Load dishwasher
- ☐ Hand-wash any larger dishes (e.g. pots and pans)
- ☐ Clean sink
- ☐ Clear and wipe benchtops
- ☐ Wipe stovetop
- ☐ Wipe splashback
- ☐ Wash microfibre cloths
- ☐ Spot-vacuum
- ☐ Pack away stray items
- ☐ Take out bins

For the dining / meals area:

- ☐ Clear dishes
- ☐ Wipe down table and chairs
- ☐ Vacuum chair upholstery
- ☐ Vacuum around and under table

CHECKLIST

- ☐ Check pantry for expired items and wipe down with multipurpose spray
- ☐ Check fridge and freezer for expired items and wipe down with fridge spray
- ☐ Clean microwave
- ☐ Clean stovetop
- ☐ Mop floors
- ☐ Clean splashbacks
- ☐ Move small appliances and wipe underneath them
- ☐ Wipe down light switches, powerpoints and doorknobs
- ☐ Wash tea towels
- ☐ Replace sponges and sponge head on your dish brush
- ☐ Wash bin and bin area
- ☐ Wash walls behind pet bowls

WEEKLY / MONTHLY KITCHEN CLEAN

- ☐ Clean kettle
- ☐ Clean toaster
- ☐ Descale coffee machine
- ☐ Clean kitchen cabinets
- ☐ Clean oven
- ☐ Clean oven warming drawer
- ☐ Clean rangehood
- ☐ Clean dishwasher
- ☐ Clear out and rinse drawer dividers and organisers
- ☐ Wipe inside cabinets
- ☐ Vacuum fridge coils
- ☐ Wipe light fixtures

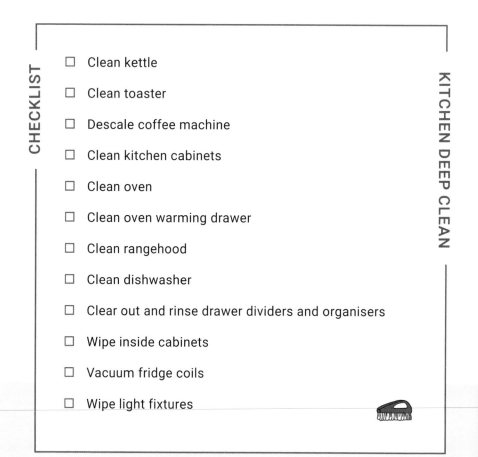

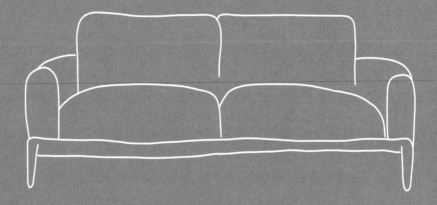

CHAPTER 2

Living room

Living rooms are just that – an area to be lived in! They're where the household comes together for a movie night, where the most competitive games of Monopoly are played, where visitors are entertained and where we unwind after a long day. The living room is a high-traffic area of the house, so we need it to be functional and beautiful in equal measure.

Before I had kids, I was one of those parents-to-be who thought I'd never let my living room become inundated with obnoxiously loud-coloured toys. How wrong I was! Fast-forward to becoming a parent – toys overflowed from every corner of our tiny home, and in the brightest shades of primary colours which contrasted so starkly with my otherwise neutral palette.

Those toys brought my kids so much joy, so of course I was happy, but a part of me felt overwhelmed by the visual clutter at the end of the day. I started looking for simple ways to balance the two worlds: a space to live and enjoy life (and this applies to other practical items like sports equipment, gaming consoles or work-from-home essentials), and a space that can look beautiful and evoke a state of calm. Throughout this chapter you'll find lots of easy, best-practice tips for decluttering everyday items.

We also need to talk about dust. Because the living room often connects different areas of the home and people pass through so often, it can become a gathering place for dust. What's more, furniture here like bookshelves, TV units and shelving have lots of nooks and crannies that can be hard to reach. Read on to find my best dusting tips and tricks, and ways to keep the dust at bay for longer.

Because the living room is so commonly used by all members of the household, everyone can take ownership. The easiest way to maintain it as a relaxing and pleasant space is to do a little bit each day and ensure the whole family is getting involved. Remember to always be kind to yourself and work around what's achievable in your day-to-day life, as everyone's routines and cleaning schedules will look a little different. Things as simple as packing away toys at the end of each night, or spot-vacuuming the room with a stick vacuum every day, can make the biggest difference.

CLEANING *playlist*

Clean in 15

The living room is where the morning rush starts, when it's often filled with toys, shoes, packed schoolbags and homework. It's also where we relax in the afternoon and evenings – imagine more toys, shoes and snacks. This is a recipe for daily clutter that can snowball out of control.

Remember in chapter 1 when we spoke about After-Dinner Time, your chance for a quick group tidy of the kitchen? The living room is a great area to add to this roster, sharing the workload within the family – kids can pack away their own toys and books, for example. In many open floor plans these two areas are close to each other, so it's easy to tackle both at the same time.

A simple daily routine is the best way to keep this area looking clean and tidy. It's the small things that make a big difference!

CHECKLIST

- ☐ Pack away electronics, remotes, blankets, toys, books and puzzles in your living room, entryway and toy / games room

- ☐ Open curtains and windows to air the room

- ☐ Spot-clean chairs, couches and upholstery

- ☐ Spot-clean carpet stains

- ☐ Vacuum carpet and rugs

- ☐ Mop floors

- ☐ Clean up entryway

WEEKLY LIVING ROOM CLEAN

DIY Upholstery Deodoriser

This spray, which you might remember from chapter 1, also works wonders to remove spot stains on your fabric couches, dining room chairs and other soft furnishings. This simple DIY has been a lifesaver in those places that are hot spots for mess and spills. Always patch-test before using this method on upholstery around your home, as every fabric is different.

You'll need:

- Spray bottle
- 1 cup soda water (carbonated water)
- ½ tsp dishwashing liquid
- Microfibre cloth

How to:

- In a spray bottle, mix soda water and dishwashing liquid.
- Spray and blot stains, then leave to dry.

Tip Lift your couch cushions and you may find a fabric swatch for your couch. Use this to patch-test cleaning products before using them on your couch!

This spray is suitable for upholstery couches. For leather couches, it's best to use a specialised leather cleaner for spot stains.

DIY Carpet and Rug Spot Cleaner

This spray will become your best friend when it comes to removing stains and spills at ground level. The acidity within the white vinegar helps cut through stains and deodorises, while the salt helps dry the stain and bring it to the surface. When cleaning carpets or rugs, always blot the stain, never rub, to avoid the spill travelling deeper into the carpet fibres. If you have thicker or more plush carpets or rugs, it's even more important to blot and not rub stains.

You'll need:

- Spray bottle
- 1 cup water
- ¼ cup white vinegar
- 2 tbsp salt
- 4–6 drops essential oil (up to personal preference, as it's for fragrance only – I like using peppermint for this mix)
- Microfibre cloth

How to:

- In a spray bottle, mix water, white vinegar, salt and essential oil.
- Shake well and spray on your carpet stains.
- Blot with a microfibre cloth until the stain is lifted.

Always patch-test on a small section before use. You can also hire a professional carpet cleaner annually to remove tough stains on your carpets and to remove any dust and dirt from deep within the fibres.

DIY Floor Cleaner

Because living rooms are high-traffic areas, they can attract a lot of dirt, mud and sand. If you have hardwood floors in this space, it's a good idea to mop them at least once a week. This mix is powerful at removing stains while still being gentle on your floors.

You'll need:

- 2 cups warm water
- 2 tsp castile soap
- 4 drops essential oil (I like to use lemon for this mix)
- Bucket and mop

How to:

- Mix water, castile soap and essential oil in a bucket.
- Mop your floors with this mixture to leave them sparkling clean.

Not all essential oils are suitable around babies and pets. You can leave out the essential oils for a fragrance-free option.

THE IMPORTANCE OF AIRING YOUR LIVING ROOM

Open your windows and doors and let the sunshine in! By ventilating your living room regularly, you can improve your air quality and rid the room of musty smells. And it's a cost-effective way to cool down or heat up your house when you need it, helping you to save on power bills!

HOW TO GET THE FAMILY INVOLVED IN ADT (AFTER-DINNER TIME)

As mentioned, the open floor plan of many modern homes allows for a continuous space between the living, dining and kitchen areas. This makes adding your living room to your household's After-Dinner Time all the more easy. Every night after dinner, when the family comes together to share the cleaning workload, assign a family member to the living room. They can do a quick tidy-up and spot-vacuum of the area to give the space a quick refresh.

HOW TO CLEAN YOUR ENTRYWAY

Because it's the gateway to your home, the entryway can collect a lot of clutter. As part of your ADTs, you can add a quick clean-up of the entryway area – each person can pick up the items that belong to them and place them in a designated place. Check out the organising section of this chapter for some storage solutions for those 'commonly dumped items' by the front door!

HOW TO CLEAN YOUR TOYS / GAMES ROOM

If you have children, or a housemate who loves to play video games, your living room or games / media room (if you have one) can quickly become a mess. Picking up toys can feel like a never-ending task, but getting your kids involved is really beneficial to you and them. When children have too many options in front of them, it can lead to overstimulation, so by tidying up toys as you go, they can focus on playing with one or two items at a time.

If your children snack in the toy area, toys can also build up germs so they'll need a quick wash before use. Occasionally toys will need a more thorough clean to get rid of germs and bacteria. Below are some ways to clean the most frequently used toys.

CLEANING ELECTRONICS AND CONSOLES
These can quickly collect dust, so wiping them down with a dry microfibre cloth every month is a great way to keep allergens away.

CLEANING PLASTIC TOYS WITHOUT ELECTRONICS
These can be washed in warm soapy water in the sink. Fill your kitchen or laundry sink up with warm water and add 1 tsp dishwashing liquid. Soak your items for about 5 minutes and rinse before air-drying. If you have small items, like Legos or doll accessories, add these to a mesh laundry bag before washing and drying to avoid any little pieces going missing.

CLEANING PLASTIC TOYS WITH ELECTRONICS

For obvious reasons, it's best to not submerge these in water. Instead, spray the DIY multipurpose spray onto a damp microfibre cloth and wipe down the toys, ensuring they don't become too wet. Wipe dry with a tea towel.

CLEANING SOFT / PLUSH TOYS

Many plush toys can be washed and dried in the washing machine on a delicate cycle, and this is a great option if your child isn't as emotionally attached to the item as it will go through a bit of a tumbling process to get clean.

If your child has a favourite soft toy or blanket they can't part with, that attachment can be very important to them, so it might be best to hand-wash the item. Fill your laundry sink with warm water and a gentle, eco-friendly detergent, preferably one that's fragrance-free. Allow the toy or blanket to soak for 15 minutes to deodorise the item, before gently washing away any spots or dirt. Rinse and air-dry.

CLEANING PLAY MATS

These are a high-contact area for kids – and pets if you have them – so regular cleaning is important to remove bacteria. The process will depend on the material:

◊ **FABRIC FLOOR MATS:** A wonderful option on carpeted floors, and many of them are washing machine safe. Check the washing instructions first, but many can be washed in cold water on a gentle cycle. Try to opt for a fragrance-free, eco-friendly detergent because this will come into close contact with your little ones' skin.

◊ **FOAM OR RUBBER FLOOR MATS:** These are what I had in my house when my kids were young. They're so durable and can be cleaned almost the same way as your regular floors, which saves so much time. When vacuuming your floors, also vacuum your foam floor mat, and when mopping your floors, you can use the same DIY floor cleaner solution (see page 71) to mop your floor mat. It's as easy as that!

CLEANING BATH TOYS / WATER TOYS

These can become a breeding ground for mould and mildew as they're used in a wet environment and are difficult to dry. Vinegar is a great natural solution to rid mould spores from toys. Simply soak bath toys in cleaning vinegar (which has a higher acidity than normal white vinegar) for 30 minutes, and if any have heavy mould, dispose of them.

Clean it *like you mean it*

As the living room is so frequently used, it's important to give it some TLC each month to remove hidden dust and allergens. Whether you're having guests over or setting up for your nightly Netflix session, there are some quick things you can do to maintain the space.

CHECKLIST

- ☐ Wipe down TV and TV unit
- ☐ Dust around the room
- ☐ Vacuum and mop floors
- ☐ Remove couch and chair cushions and throw blankets, and wash them
- ☐ Vacuum curtains and/or wipe blinds
- ☐ Wipe down windowsills and tracks
- ☐ Disinfect your remote control and electronic gadgets

MONTHLY LIVING ROOM CLEAN

DIY Dusting Spray

This spray is perfect for wooden furniture around the home where dust seems to accumulate, like coffee tables, TV units and side tables, along with bedsides, dressers and tallboys. This mix contains a small amount of oil that coats your furniture and prevents dust from settling on it for longer.

You'll need:

- Spray bottle
- 1 cup water
- ¼ cup white vinegar
- 4 drops lemon essential oil
- 2 tbsp fractionated coconut oil (or melted coconut oil)

How to:

- Mix the water, white vinegar and oils in a spray bottle, then shake to combine.
- Spray on your furniture, then wipe with a damp microfibre cloth. As always, patch-test before use.

WHAT IS FRACTIONATED COCONUT OIL?

This oil, also known as liquid coconut oil, is made by separating the different fats in coconut oil to give more of a liquid consistency that doesn't harden. You can find this at your local supermarket.

◊ **First, clear the clutter**. Dusting can seem like a never-ending task, but the fewer things you have in your living room, the less dust will accumulate. Remove all the objects from flat surfaces to make your job easier.

◊ A note on equipment: say goodbye to the good old feather duster! These are actually ineffective at removing dust from your home – instead of capturing the dust, they can shift it around. **It's more helpful to dust with a damp microfibre cloth and the DIY dusting spray. This process is called damp dusting.**

◊ Before you begin, make sure you dust the right way! **Always start from the top and work your way down.** This way, as the dust falls downwards, you can collect it. Wait a few minutes for dust to settle before moving on to the next section.

◊ **Move the big items.** As tempting as it may be to dust around your heavy furniture, like your couch or rugs, a lot of the allergens and dust can be lurking behind or beneath them. Pull your furniture out of the way and vacuum and dust underneath them to remove hidden dust.

◊ **Don't forget your TV.** The screen of your TV and the area behind it can accumulate a lot of dust, so don't forget to wipe it down before you vacuum the room. While you're there, also give your console a quick wipe-down with a dry microfibre cloth.

◊ **Don't forget soft furnishings.** Couches, curtains and chairs can harbour hidden dust, so vacuuming these items at least monthly helps keep that dust away.

◊ **Don't forget house plants.** Wipe the leaves of your house plants with a dry microfibre cloth monthly to keep dust away. This also helps them thrive as it allows them to absorb more sunlight.

◊ Finally, **finish with a thorough vacuum of the area.** Wait 10 minutes for any dust in the air to settle, then vacuum it all up.

HOW TO CLEAN WINDOWSILLS AND DOOR TRACKS

Windowsills and door tracks should be wiped down regularly to remove any dirt and dust that's collected. Simply use the DIY multipurpose spray with microfibre cloth on these areas to remove hidden build-up. You can also use a toothbrush to get into any tight nooks and crannies and then wipe down the area with a microfibre cloth.

To clean window tracks around the window opening, there's a simple trick you can use. Lay a flat sponge on your window railing and note with a marker where the tracks are. Using scissors, gently slice the sponge lengthways where the tracks would sit, without cutting all the way through. The sponge will now clean perfectly along your window or door tracks.

HOW TO WASH THROWS

Throws on your couch often get much dirtier than throws on your bed because they're used more often and attract mess from shoes, food and drinks. Here's a simple method to wash throws when they need it:

◊ Check the care instructions of your throw.

◊ Place in your washing machine and add gentle laundry detergent.

◊ Add 2–3 drops eucalyptus or tea-tree oil to help remove dustmites and spot stains.

◊ Wash on the warmest setting your throw allows.

◊ Dry as per the care instructions.

HOW TO WASH CUSHION COVERS

A quick and easy way to refresh your living room is to clean your cushions and make the entire space more cosy and inviting. Whether your cushions have food or drink stains, or are just in need of a bit of TLC, it's very easy to give them a refresh.

◊ Remove cushions from their pillowcase and read the care instructions on the inner tag.

◊ Place cushion covers in your washing machine and add a gentle laundry detergent.

◊ Add 2–3 drops eucalyptus or tea-tree oil to help remove dust mites and spot stains.

◊ Wash on the warmest setting your pillowcase care instructions allow.

◊ Dry as per the care instructions.

When washing your cushion covers, don't forget the pillows themselves. While you wash your cushion covers, use a handheld vacuum with an upholstery attachment to vacuum your inner pillows. The pillows don't need frequent washing, but every year it's good to place them in the washing machine (if the care instructions allow) to remove dustmites and keep them fresh. Dry them flat in the shade, then when they're nearly dry, place in the dryer for 10 minutes with a dryer ball (see chapter 5) to make them fluffy.

HOW TO DISINFECT YOUR REMOTES AND ELECTRONIC GADGETS

Remote controls are an often overlooked area, but high-frequency contact by different household members means they can be a breeding ground for germs. To remove dirt and dust, slightly dampen a microfibre cloth then spray the controller with the DIY multipurpose spray and wipe it down.

Deep *clean*

Now that your living room has a regular routine, it will be much easier to manage the clutter to make the process less stressful. The deep-cleaning tasks below are just a little bit of extra TLC to get those hard-to-reach places in order. They can be done seasonally or annually, based on your household's needs.

CHECKLIST

- ☐ Dust ceiling fans and lights
- ☐ Remove all items from bookshelves, TV units and hutches and wipe them
- ☐ Vacuum curtains and wipe blinds
- ☐ Remove curtains and wash them
- ☐ Clean air conditioner filters
- ☐ Clean walls and baseboards
- ☐ Steam-clean carpets and rugs
- ☐ Vacuum under couch and rugs
- ☐ Move large furniture items and vacuum under them
- ☐ Clean vacuum cleaner filters

HOW TO DUST CEILING FANS AND LIGHTS

Ceilings fans can be an 'out of sight, out of mind' area of the home. After not using them during winter, dust and allergens can build up on the blades, which is then dispersed around the room when the fan is switched on. Before the weather starts warming up is the perfect time to clean them.

Did you know that ceiling fans can be cleaned using a pillowcase? Simply place each fan blade inside a pillowcase, then use the pillowcase to wipe the blade. The dust gets trapped inside the pillowcase and can be placed directly into the washing machine to wash all that dust away!

HOW TO CLEAN BOOKSHELVES AND TV UNITS

Bookshelves are a great vertical storage solution, but they can also build up a lot of dust. Unfortunately, there are no shortcuts to getting rid of that – but here's a quick step-by-step:

◊ Empty just the top shelf to begin with.

◊ Use the crevice tool on your vacuum cleaner to vacuum, then wipe down with the DIY dusting spray.

◊ Replace the items then move to the shelf below, working your way downwards.

◊ As a bonus tip, if you have very tall bookshelves and struggle to clean the top of them, try lining the top with old newspaper. This way, the dust settles on the newspaper and can be switched out quickly and easily.

HOW TO CLEAN CURTAINS

The easiest way to clean your curtains is to vacuum them to remove the dust and allergens in the fibres. Start at the top and work your way towards the bottom. If your curtains are in need of a wash, start by checking the care instructions on the tag then wash them accordingly.

Any curtains with block-out features must be washed in cold water only and should be dried flat in the shade. The coated, block-out fabric can become sticky when wet, and can stick and tear if not dried flat.

HOW TO CLEAN BLINDS

Did you know you can use kitchen tongs to make this process easier? Wrap a microfibre cloth around each side of the tongs then secure with a rubber band. Use to clean each slat of your blinds – you'll be able to clean both sides of the slats at the same time. Too easy!

HOW TO CLEAN AIR CONDITIONER FILTERS

Check your manual for the best way to remove the filters so you can vacuum and wipe them down. This will remove the dust and also make the machine more efficient, which can help reduce your power bills.

WHY YOU SHOULD STEAM-CLEAN YOUR CARPETS AND RUGS

This is a great way to remove hidden odours from your home and leave these well-worn surfaces smelling fresh, but it also has many other benefits. The hot water extraction from steam cleaning removes allergens from your carpets, removes stains and cleans deep into the carpet fibres in a way that spot-cleaning is unable to.

You have 2 options here – you can get a professional carpet cleaner in once a year, or many places offer carpet cleaner machine hire, which is a much more cost-effective option!

HOW TO CLEAN WALLS AND BASEBOARDS

This sounds like a time-consuming and labour-intensive task, but there's a simple and fast method that will save your back from all that bending – a flat microfibre mop is the lifesaver here. Cleaning your walls leaves your entire home smelling amazing, though always patch-test to make sure the paint on your walls is washable.

You'll need:

- Bucket
- 2 cups water
- 1 tbsp dishwashing liquid
- 4–5 drops essential oil (optional – this is purely for fragrance, so it depends on your preferences)
- Microfibre mop

How to:

- In a bucket, mix water, dishwashing liquid and essential oil if you choose.
- Using a clean microfibre mop that's damp but not fully wet, apply the mixture to the walls. In long motions, run the mop up and down to clean them with ease.
- This same method can be used to clean baseboards quickly and easily.

Tip If your walls are quite dusty, first use a dry microfibre cloth to dislodge loose dust.

PLACES EVERYONE FORGETS TO CLEAN IN THE LIVING ROOM

Underneath rugs and furniture: What's hiding under your couch? If you find your living room gets dusty frequently, places like this could be the culprit. When wind blows through the living room, dust hiding in these spaces may end up blowing through the room. To combat this, simply move your furniture and clean behind and underneath seasonally.

Tops of bookshelves, tall shelving and picture frames: The next time you're dusting your living room, don't forget to look to the top! These are common places where dust can collect. You can use a damp microfibre mop to clean quickly and gently (and be sure to remove any cobwebs while you're up there!).

Vacuum filters: Don't forget to clean the items that clean your home! Most vacuums have a filter that should be washed seasonally, and these can often be washed in warm, soapy water then air-dried. Also check your vacuum head for any blockages, and clear hair or debris from the brush head.

Lightbulbs and lamps: If you have a lamp in your living room, when was the last time you wiped the bulb? It's a simple, quick task that will make your lamp shine brighter. And to clean your lampshade, you can use a lint roller – simply roll it across to pick up dust easily!

Indoor plants: Whether you have real or faux indoor plants, dust can collect on the leaves. Simply take a damp microfibre cloth and run it across them. If you have real plants, you can even pop them into the shower and give them a thorough water and rinse all at once!

DEEP-CLEANING YOUR *home office*

Depending on your work routines, we can spend a lot of time here during the day. If your desk is filled with clutter and paperwork, it can be hard to find what you're looking for and the space can make it difficult to concentrate. Many of us also eat at our desks, so spills, crumbs and mess can be part of the territory.

If your home office could do with a refresh, here are some simple tips that can help you create a beautiful and clutter-free space:

◊ Take everything off your desk and wipe down the non-electronic equipment with the DIY multipurpose cleaner.

◊ Dust your computer, mouse, phone headsets and any other electronic equipment with a dry microfibre cloth. Although damp-dusting is very effective, it's obviously best to play it safe by dry-dusting your electronics!

◊ Turn your keyboard upside down and use a sticky note to clean in between the keys. This is a simple trick to remove dust from the tight spaces. If you don't have sticky notes, a compressed-air spray or a cotton bud also works well.

◊ If you have any hard-to-remove water rings on your desk, use a hairdryer to heat the rings for one minute before wiping them down.

◊ Sort through paper clutter and get rid of things you don't need. You can categorise items into three piles:
  - Declutter items you no longer need that can be thrown away or recycled.
  - Organise items that you need, to be filed away in their respective spots.
  - Action items that require immediate action before filing, like bills.

◊ Empty any bookshelves in the office and wipe each shelf from top to bottom before placing items back on it.

◊ Empty and replace the bin.

◊ Once you've finished cleaning the items in your home office, wait 10 minutes for the dust to settle and give the whole room a thorough vacuum to get rid of dust.

Entryway

Keeping this space clean and tidy allows you to welcome yourself home with a clutter-free space, and to make a great first impression on visitors. The reality is that the entryway can become a dumping ground for shoes, bags, paperwork and mail, so here are some simple tips to create a beautiful and functional entryway for all family members.

Wipe down your front door: Give it a quick wipe with the DIY multipurpose spray to remove marks.

Remove cobwebs: Use a dry mop to remove any cobwebs from hard-to-reach spaces, and don't forget the area above your front door.

Clean the welcome mat: Wipe your entire doorframe of bugs and cobwebs, then shake your welcome mat to dislodge stuck dirt and spray it with a hose. While you've got the hose out, give your potted plants at your entryway some water too!

Dust furniture: Once you walk through the front door, remove all items from your hallway console table and wipe it with a damp microfibre cloth to remove dust.

Take items to their respective rooms: As the front door area can become cluttered with items from other rooms, return them to their rightful places and think about ways to avoid them piling up in the same area again. For example, if you find your front entry is cluttered with schoolbags, adding a few hooks to the wall could be a simple way to create a 'home' for them. If the space is cluttered with shoes, a shoe storage cabinet may be called for. If there is a lot of clutter that belongs in multiple rooms or to different household members, compile them into separate baskets for everyone to sort through themselves.

Vacuum the floor: Now that the area is clean and clutter-free, wait 10 minutes for dust to settle before vacuuming and mopping the floor to remove germs and bacteria.

See page 90 for tips to organise your entryway!

Organising

So many fun family moments are created in the living room. It's the place where we have movie nights, entertain friends, spend lazy Sundays and where the kids play their favourite games. And this means it can get very messy very quickly. Keeping on top of the mess through an organising system will not only make all of your cleaning routines much easier, it will also make the space more relaxing – a place where you can really live!

LIVING ROOM ORGANISING TIPS AND TRICKS:

Declutter and donate: Keep only the items you love and use regularly. When decluttering, a quick rule of thumb is to ask yourself, 'If I saw this at a second-hand store, would I purchase it?' If the answer is no, then it may be time to donate that item.

Follow the 'one in, one out' shopping strategy: If you're like me and love buying new homewares and décor, this rule is for you! If you're buying an item that you don't currently have a 'home' for, or if it's a duplicate, you must promise yourself to donate or declutter another item. This strategy can be used with clothing, homewares or any purchase to avoid overspending and decrease clutter.

Functional furniture and storage: Once you've narrowed down your items to what you actually use and love, it's time to think about storage. Maximise your living room space with functional furniture like a coffee table with hidden storage space – this could be used to keep magazines, remotes and books. A modular couch with hidden storage can be used to store extra throws and pillows. These are all great ways to find hidden 'homes' for important items that otherwise contribute to visual clutter.

Vertical storage: Bookshelves are also a great storage area! Add baskets and trays to categorise items and keep the room looking neat and tidy.

Ottomans with storage for toy boxes: Instead of a large toy box, opt for a large padded storage ottoman that matches your living-room décor. At the end of the day when the toys are packed away, the area still feels like an adult space for you to relax in. Just make sure whatever option you choose is friendly to little fingers who will also use it.

Baskets: These are your best friend in the living room. Different-sized baskets can be used all around the living room as a 'home' to organise various items like electronics, toys, throws, cushions, paperwork, keys and knick-knacks. Each household member could have their own small basket to keep their own gadgets in, or you could have a communal one for all gadgets.

Cords, wires and chargers: If these take up a lot of space in your home, having a separate basket for them can be very useful. You can even use empty toilet rolls to store each charger in, to make sure they don't get tangled. Roll each phone charger and place them in individual toilet rolls to ensure they don't get tangled together.

HOW TO ORGANISE YOUR ENTRYWAY

Create a entryway drop zone: Schoolbags, handbags, laptop bags and backpacks can take up a lot of space here. Creating a dedicated drop zone at your front door, using cube shelving, a large bookshelf or a console table, can be the perfect way to have all this clutter in one place.

Shoe organisation: Shoes are the other big culprit here. Taking your shoes off before entering the home is an important way to reduce dust, dirt and allergens, so to encourage this behaviour in household members and guests, and to keep things in order, add a shoe rack or similar near the front door.

Keys, loose change and sunglasses: How often have you been trying to rush outside and you can't find one of these? Creating a dedicated space by the entryway – like a basket, drawer or even old candle jars – will minimise clutter and save you from last-minute panics before you head out.

UPCYCLE YOUR USED CANDLE JARS
The next time you finish your candles, don't throw away the container. Place the jar in the freezer for a few hours, then use a blunt knife to gently lift the excess wax from the bottom of the jar and remove the wicks. Use eucalyptus oil on a cotton ball to remove any labels on the jar. Wash the jar in warm, soapy water and you now have a great, reusable jar for your keys and change!

Styling

A well-styled living room can make such a big difference. Remember, it's all about balance – the goal in revamping your living room is to create a beautiful and practical space that you are proud to entertain your guests in, but also one that you can relax in at the end of the day. When choosing your style, think about the places that bring you joy and incorporate colours from your favourite places, photos of your family and friends, candles that bring scents you love into your home, and/or books that bring you joy and peace.

THINK ABOUT YOUR LIVING-ROOM COLOUR SCHEME
This tip is not for every household, but can be very useful if you have a living room filled with lots of loud-coloured toys (like my house!). If this is you, my advice is to stick with a neutral colour palette to reduce visual clutter. When your kids are playing with their toys and the space is filled with pops of colour, the neutral background makes the room look cleaner and more streamlined.

HOW TO STYLE YOUR COFFEE TABLE
When styling any furniture item around the home, think about the rule of thirds, which says that items look best when clustered into groups of 3s, 6s or 9s. Start by placing down an 'anchor' – this could be a tray or your favourite book (you can use this book!) – then add 3 of your favourite décor items on the top. This could be a candle, a slim vase or a small dish. Books are of course wonderful items to display on your coffee table – they look great, and they're excellent conversation-starters.

When clustering these groups of décor around your home, think about mixing heights, textures and colours, and adding a pop of real or faux greenery. You can also add a tray to your coffee table as a place to keep your remote controls or electronic gadgets so they're organised and neat.

HOW TO HANG YOUR PICTURE FRAMES

When hanging picture frames or photographs it can be tricky to get the frames straight every time, especially if you have hooks on either side. There can be confusing calculations, guesswork or, even worse, a process of trial and error that leaves holes in your walls.

Luckily, there's a simple trick to help hang your pictures straight every single time! Simply place masking tape or painter's tape on the back of your artwork and mark where the hooks should be placed on the tape. Place the tape on your wall and make sure it's level. Place your holes into the wall using the markings on the tape as a guide. Peel off the tape and hang your artwork perfectly straight.

HOW TO STYLE YOUR TV UNIT

We spend a lot of time looking at the TV each day, so making the area around it visually pleasing is a great way to help make your downtime even more enjoyable and relaxing. Here are some tips and tricks:

◊ **Wall-mounting:** This can make your living room space look larger as the TV's cords are concealed and you get more visual flow. You can also mount your TV to swivel so it faces different directions.

◊ **Paint the wall behind black:** A simple way to conceal your TV when switched off. This won't suit every home's decor, but is a great, chic solution for some styles.

◊ **Place your TV next to another element that draws the eye:** This could be a large potted plant or painting that avoids the TV becoming the focal point of the room.

◊ **Add rounded elements beside it:** This will balance the harsh lines of the appliance. You can include, for example, plants, table lamps or candle-holders.

HOW TO STYLE YOUR COUCH

When choosing your couch, opting for a neutral colour can save you money down the track. Instead of creating a feature piece with your couch, create your feature with less expensive items like cushions and throws in different textures, patterns and shapes. You can switch these out easily as seasons and trends change, while still keeping your couch as the base.

Like other areas of the home, think about the colours and textures that make you feel most relaxed and bring you joy. This is an area where personality and flair thrive, so add your own personal touch.

HOW TO CHOOSE A RUG FOR YOUR LIVING ROOM

Rugs can be a large investment, so buying the one that's right for your room is so important. The layout of your living room helps determine what size rug would work best, but as a rule of thumb, rugs should be large enough to run the entire width of your couch and wide enough to be placed under the front two legs of the couch and cover your space.

Rugs that are too small for a space can make a room appear smaller than they actually are, so bigger is often better. If you prefer small rugs, try placing it under one item only to create a focal piece, like under your coffee table or under a feature armchair.

Before you buy your rug, use painter's tape or masking tape to mark the area of the rug on the floor to give you a feel for the size before purchase! Fabric samples are also great to see the colours of the rug in your space, as homes have different lighting to stores, so the colours can look different in each space.

REAL VS FAUX *plants?*

This is simply a question of personal preference and both options have their own benefits, but either way, plants can add effortless style to any space, whether it's a large potted plant in the corner of a room or a hanging plant in your bathroom. They add a great pop of colour and help bring the feeling of the outside world into your home.

Faux plants have changed a lot in the last few years, and there are some great, affordable options which look very realistic. The benefit of faux plants is that they are very low maintenance and can be placed anywhere in the home without having to worry about sunlight placement. They're a great alternative if you have small children and want to avoid mud or soil inside the home.

Real plants are also a wonderful addition to the home, with physical and mental health benefits including improved air quality and helping to reduce stress levels.

STYLING THE FRONT *entryway*

The furniture you choose here will depend on the space itself and your household structure – for example, how many people live in your home, what sports or activities you play and whether you have children living in the home. A popular option for entryways is a console table, great for storing everyday items, with a mirror over the top.

If you require more storage for schoolbags or sports equipment, consider a multi-level bookshelf or cube shelving to create a 'drop zone' for items you need throughout the week. And if you're low on space, a simple row of hooks on the wall to hang jackets, hats and bags may be all that's needed to keep the area clear and clutter-free.

Did you know you can colour-code your keys using nail polish? If you find yourself fumbling for the right key to your front door, back doors and security gates, simply use nail polish to colour in the tops of your keys!

Living room routines and checklists

- ☐ Pack away electronics, remotes, blankets, toys, books and puzzles in your living room, entryway and toy / games room

- ☐ Open curtains and windows to air the room

- ☐ Spot-clean chairs, couches and upholstery

- ☐ Spot-clean carpet stains

- ☐ Vacuum carpet and rugs

- ☐ Mop floors

- ☐ Clean up entryway

WEEKLY LIVING ROOM CLEAN

CHECKLIST

- ☐ Wipe down TV and TV unit
- ☐ Dust around the room
- ☐ Vacuum and mop floors
- ☐ Remove couch and chair cushions and throw blankets, and wash them
- ☐ Vacuum curtains and/or wipe blinds
- ☐ Wipe down windowsills and tracks
- ☐ Disinfect your remote control and electronic gadgets

MONTHLY LIVING ROOM CLEAN

CHECKLIST

- ☐ Dust ceiling fans and lights
- ☐ Remove all items from bookshelves, TV units and hutches and wipe them
- ☐ Vacuum curtains and wipe blinds
- ☐ Remove curtains and wash them
- ☐ Clean air conditioner filters
- ☐ Clean walls and baseboards
- ☐ Steam-clean carpets and rugs
- ☐ Vacuum under couch and rugs
- ☐ Move large furniture items and vacuum under them
- ☐ Clean vacuum cleaner filters

LIVING ROOM DEEP CLEAN

CHAPTER 3

Bedroom

If you live with other people, whether in a family home or a share house, **your bedroom can be your oasis away from the noise, a space that's all yours**. Because it's also where you start and finish your day, keeping it clean and clutter-free is so important. The good news is that **the bedroom is a quick and easy area of the room to keep clean,** and it's not difficult (or expensive!) to add those small touches that will create a pleasant, even luxurious space.

There's no feeling quite like climbing into a bed with fresh, crisp linen. **Clean sheets and a clean room always bring a sense of comfort and warmth.** When I was younger and I would come back from a sleepover or a school camp, my mum would always surprise me and my siblings with freshly washed sheets. It was such a simple display of affection.

There's a famous saying that if you want to change the world, start by making your bed. This idea speaks to the small, simple habit changes we can make to get our days off to the right start. There's a snowball effect: doing something productive like making your bed helps you feel more confident to tackle the next, larger task, and then the next. When I moved out of home, taking the couple of minutes to make my bed every morning helped to quickly change my daily routine and mindset about cleaning. And even these days, I encourage my kids to get involved with making their own beds, to teach them from a young age the importance of a clean space.

Taking things to the next level, **a well-styled bedroom is a simple way to add a luxurious feel to your home**. Start by thinking about your favourite place: it might be the beach, the snow, the forest or even your childhood home. Think about the colours and feelings of this space, then weave in those subtle influences throughout your bedroom. If your favourite place is the countryside, you could incorporate forest greens and sage bed linens and earthy décor items. If your favourite space is the beach, you could add sand-coloured sheets and white coral décor to your bedsides.

It doesn't have to be a literal interpretation of the space – simply use colours, textures and symbols to **create a space where you can start and end your day in your most relaxed mindset possible.**

In this chapter you'll find simple, practical and inexpensive ways to help make your bedroom a place that will be so cosy you may never want to leave!

CLEANING *playlist*

Clean IN 15

Small changes to your daily bedroom cleaning routine can have instant results. When your bedroom is clean and organised, you don't need to worry about being late for work or getting the kids to school on time because you're trying to track down your clothes and accessories! All it takes is a few minutes per day to keep your bedroom in order, and you'll buy that time back and then some.

DAILY BEDROOM CLEAN

CHECKLIST

- ☐ Make bed
- ☐ Clear cups and other clutter from bedsides
- ☐ Put away clothes in wardrobe
- ☐ Place dirty clothes in laundry basket
- ☐ Keep outfits ready and bags packed for next morning
- ☐ Change and wash pillowcase every 3–4 days

CHECKLIST

- ☐ Make beds
- ☐ Pack up toys
- ☐ Place dirty clothes in laundry basket
- ☐ Pack away homework
- ☐ Keep clean uniforms, clean shoes and bags packed ready for next morning

DAILY KIDS' BEDROOM CLEAN

HOW TO WASH YOUR PILLOWCASE

Pillowcases build up sweat, oils, dirt and skin cells which can lead to breakouts and collect allergen particles. When I was a young teenager I battled with acne, and it wasn't until my mid-20s that I was able to get it under control – one of the simplest fixes was washing my pillowcase more frequently, every 3–4 days. If you don't have time to wash them that frequently, you can simply switch one pillowcase out for another and then wash them in your bigger weekend clean.

You'll need:
- Laundry detergent
- 2–3 drops eucalyptus oil

How to:
- Place pillowcases in your washing machine along with laundry detergent and eucalyptus oil.
- Wash on a gentle cycle, then dry as usual.

Washing your pillowcase and top sheet regularly is a quick and easy way to save time and reduce the frequency that your linen needs to be washed. Instead of washing your full linens weekly, you can replace your pillowcase and top sheet weekly, then stretch your full linen change to every fortnight.

Tip Adding eucalyptus oil to your wash helps to get rid of dustmites and allergens.

DIY Linen Spray

Make your bedroom smell like a dream by spritzing this spray on your bed daily after making it, or just before you go to sleep for a peaceful slumber. You can also use it on your pyjamas or as a more general room spray.

You'll need:

- ⅓ cup distilled water
- 10 drops essential oil of your choice
- 2 tsp witch hazel (This helps the oil to mix with the water. Substitutes for this are 2 tsp vodka or 2 tsp isopropyl / rubbing alcohol.)
- Small spray bottle (approx 80ml)

How to:

- Simply mix the water, oil and witch hazel together in the bottle, then spray as you please!

Distilled water is a pure form of water that has gone through the distillation process to remove the salt, fluoride and chlorine that can be present in tap water. You can find it at most supermarkets. It's recommended in this spray to avoid the spray leaving water spots on your linen, but if you don't have distilled water, you can use tap water in this mix.

Bedroom Scents You can customise the DIY linen spray with your very own blend of essential oils. Below are some of my favourite blends:

- ◊ **Relaxing:** lavender + ylang ylang
- ◊ **Uplifting:** lemon + tangerine + pine + bergamot
- ◊ **Fresh:** lavender + peppermint

DIY Wrinkle Release Spray

This simple DIY spray is a must-have! Simply spray on your linen to reduce wrinkles, or on your clothes to save time on ironing. The hair conditioner helps to soften the fibres that release wrinkles on clothes and linens. Always make sure you patch-test on the fabric before use.

You'll need:

- 2 cups water
- 1 tbsp hair conditioner
- Spray bottle

How to:

- Mix water and hair conditioner in spray bottle.
- Spray a light mist on your fabric, smooth it and leave for 5 minutes to dry.

Tip

———

This spray is wonderful to make for travelling, to help reduce wrinkles on clothes that have been tightly packed in a suitcase. Simply place hair conditioner in a small spray bottle and top up with water once you reach your destination!

TIPS AND TRICKS *for a* TIDIER BEDROOM

If you or anyone in your household struggles to keep their bedroom tidy – I'm looking at your kids! – an easy fix is to bring in new organisational systems. Here are some tips to prevent floor clutter:

◊   Keep a basket in your room for dirty clothes to avoid them collecting on the ground. You can make this basket part of your room décor by opting for a wicker or woven basket that suits the colour scheme.

◊   Create a space for clothes that are too dirty for the wardrobe but too clean for the wash. This could be a small hanging rack or chair.

◊   Look at which items are 'commonly dumped' in your bedroom – it's usually things like clothes, bags and shoes. Create 'homes' around your bedroom for these items, so you can put them away. This may be hooks on the back of your door to hang your bag or a tray to keep loose change and keys.

◊   If you're lacking space in your bedroom, think about decluttering items. A simple rule of thumb when decluttering is to think, 'If I saw this at a shop, would I purchase it?' If the answer is no, it may be time to donate it or place it in storage.

◊   Make your bed every day as part of your morning routine. I know I'm repeating myself here, but it's an easy way to make your bedroom tidier!

TIPS AND TRICKS TO HELP KEEP *kids' rooms* TIDIER

Keeping kids' rooms tidy can be a tricky job, especially when you hear responses like 'But why?!' and 'I don't want to!' But it's important to persevere – the earlier that kids start cleaning their room and taking responsibility for their own space, the better.

Play music
A simple trick to get kids to make their beds each morning is to play their favourite 2-minute song while they make their bed and they'll be done before it ends. They'll come to understand how quick and easy the job is, and it's a chance to create fun family memories.

Start a rewards chart
A simple sticker chart in a communal space, like the kitchen fridge, is a perfect way to motivate kids, reinforce their good behaviour and build confidence.

Create an 'entry drop zone'
This is a dedicated area for shoes, bags, homework, newsletters and sports equipment to go when kids return home from school. Use cube shelving or a large bookshelf to put these commonly dumped items in one place and keep kids' rooms tidier.

GUEST *bedroom*

Because the guest bedroom isn't used often, it's an easy place to keep clean and neat. Here's a simple checklist to prepare for a guest staying with you:

◊ Change linens.

◊ Remove any items that belong in other rooms.

◊ Wipe down bedsides using the DIY dusting spray (see page 114).

◊ Vacuum floors and bedhead.

If you want to really take things to the next level and treat your guest/s like royalty, you can do any of the following:

◊ Roll towels and place at the base of the bed – a small hotel-style touch!

◊ Use the DIY linen spray on the sheets.

◊ To really go above and beyond, you can make a small welcome hamper including a mini body wash, shampoo, conditioner, deodorant, mouthwash, floss, chocolates and/or toothbrush.

CLEAN IT *like you mean it*

A 'fresh sheet Sunday' routine is a wonderful start to the week! There is such a therapeutic element to stripping off linens then washing away a week's worth of dirt, sweat, dead skin cells and dustmites to start the next week fresh and clean. And there's no better form of self-care than a great night's sleep, which can be so restorative for the body and mind. Build these weekly and monthly routines into your schedule to transform your room into a place of rejuvenation and calm.

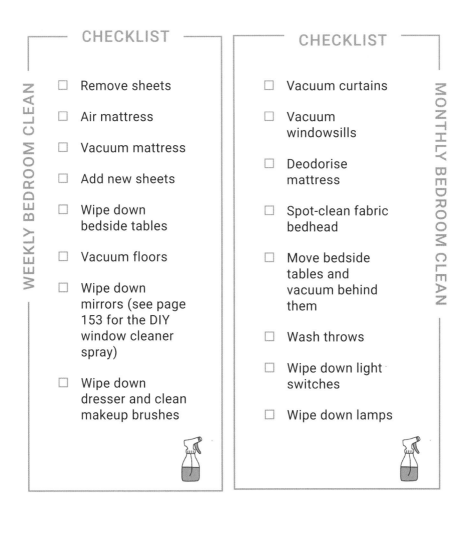

WEEKLY BEDROOM CLEAN

CHECKLIST

- ☐ Remove sheets
- ☐ Air mattress
- ☐ Vacuum mattress
- ☐ Add new sheets
- ☐ Wipe down bedside tables
- ☐ Vacuum floors
- ☐ Wipe down mirrors (see page 153 for the DIY window cleaner spray)
- ☐ Wipe down dresser and clean makeup brushes

MONTHLY BEDROOM CLEAN

CHECKLIST

- ☐ Vacuum curtains
- ☐ Vacuum windowsills
- ☐ Deodorise mattress
- ☐ Spot-clean fabric bedhead
- ☐ Move bedside tables and vacuum behind them
- ☐ Wash throws
- ☐ Wipe down light switches
- ☐ Wipe down lamps

MATTRESS *maintenance*

What's hiding in your mattress? These can become breeding grounds for allergens, dustmites, dead skin cells, bacteria and sweat, but they're also frequently overlooked. Regular mattress TLC is important for a great night's sleep.

Mattress rotations

Some mattresses need to be rotated every 6–12 months to preserve their shape and avoid indenting or sagging where we sleep. To rotate your mattress, simply turn it around from head to foot, and flip it upside down if it's double sided. Some mattresses are not designed to be rotated (like customised mattresses where each person has a custom zone), so it's best to check the care instructions first.

Why should we air our mattress?

All mattresses should be aired once a week to avoid musty smells, bacteria and odours, and to prevent mould forming within them. Remove all bedding and sheets then open your curtains and windows to allow the mattress to air for half an hour – you can do this while your bedding is in the washing machine.

Why should we vacuum our mattress?

Once your mattress has finished airing, run a hand vacuum across it, with the upholstery attachment, to remove the dust, dustmites and germs lurking within it. Don't forget to also vacuum your bedhead, bedside tables and flooring around the bed while you're at it.

Mattress protectors and mattress toppers

Using a waterproof mattress protector underneath your fitted sheet is a great way to keep your mattress clean, as are mattress toppers. These are thicker and more plush, similar to a quilt. Toppers also provide an extra layer of comfort if your mattress is older or uncomfortable.

DIY Dustmite Spray / Mattress Deodoriser Spray

Dustmites love moist environments and live off human skin cells, so they live where you spend the most time – in your bed! Applying this mattress spray weekly after you vacuum your mattress can help remove dustmites from your personal space.

You'll need:

- ½ cup water
- ½ cup white vinegar
- 10 drops lavender oil
- 10 drops peppermint oil
- 10 drops eucalyptus oil
- Spray bottle

How to:

- Mix water, white vinegar and oils in spray bottle, then shake to combine.
- Simply spray a light mist on your mattress, bedhead or any upholstered items around your home.

What are dustmites?

Dustmites are microscopic organisms, part of the spider family, and are present in nearly every household. They commonly live in mattresses, bedding, carpets and upholstered bedheads and couches. Fortunately, as they are microscopic, we cannot see them and they do not bite, but they can cause allergy symptoms and skin irritations. Washing bedding in hot water frequently, regularly vacuuming soft furnishings and decluttering your space are simple ways to reduce dustmites around your home and in your bedroom.

HOW TO WASH YOUR BEDSHEETS

On average, bedsheets should be washed once a week, especially if you have a pet that sleeps with you or if you have dust allergies or asthma. If your allergies worsen over spring, washing your sheets on an even more frequent basis can help reduce allergens in your home. Before you wash, check the care instructions of your sheets, as every material is different!

◊ Place linens in your washing machine and add a gentle laundry detergent into the detergent tray.

◊ Add ½ cup baking soda directly to the drum of your machine. This is optional – it'll help to soften and deodorise your sheets.

◊ Wash on the warmest setting your sheets allow.

◊ Dry as per the care instructions.

> If you don't want to wash your sheets every week, you can have a few bed linen options – say, 2–3 sets – on rotation. Some prefer to have many, many more sets to switch out the look, feel and colour scheme of your bedroom. It's completely up to you!

HOW TO CARE FOR YOUR BED LINENS

It's always best to check the care instructions on your sheets before washing them. Here are some simple washing and drying tips for the most common fabrics:

Cotton sheets: Can generally be washed on a warm-water setting on a normal cycle. Line-dry in the shade or tumble-dry on a medium heat.

Linen sheets: Should be washed in cold or warm water on a gentle cycle. Line-dry in the shade. If they go a bit stiff, you can place them in the dryer on the coolest setting for 5–10 minutes with a dryer ball (see chapter 5) to help soften them.

Flannelette sheets: To prevent these from shedding or balling, wash with your normal detergent and 1 cup white vinegar in the fabric softener compartment for the first load. After the first wash, wash on a warm-water setting on a delicate cycle, then line-dry in the shade.

Silk sheets: These need a lot of care. You can wash silk in a delicate garment bag on a delicate cycle, or by hand. Turn pillowcases inside out and wash with a gentle silk detergent. Line-dry only.

HOW TO WASH YOUR THROWS AND BLANKETS

Because these are usually layered on top of your bed, they don't get as dirty as your sheets. They can be placed in the washing machine every 3–4 months, or more often if you have a pet or allergies. As with your sheets, check the care instructions of the fabric before you wash!

◊ Place throw in your washing machine and add a gentle laundry detergent.

◊ Add 2–3 drops eucalyptus, lavender or peppermint oil to your laundry detergent to help remove dustmites.

◊ Wash on the warmest setting your throw allows.

◊ Dry as per the care instructions.

DIY Dusting Spray

This spray may look familiar as it's the same one you can use in your living room! In the bedroom, this spray can be used in places where dust accumulates, like bedsides, dressers, tallboys, TV units and coffee tables.

You'll need:
- 1 cup water
- ¼ cup white vinegar
- 4 drops lemon essential oil
- 2 tbsp fractionated coconut oil (or melted coconut oil)
- Spray bottle

How to:
- Mix the water, white vinegar and oils in spray bottle, then shake to combine.
- Spray on your furniture, then wipe with a damp microfibre cloth. As always, patch-test before use.

Benefits of damp dusting A common frustration when dusting the home is sneezing and itchy eyes. An easy way to combat this is to slightly dampen your dusting cloth with water or the DIY dusting spray. The dust sticks to the cloth rather than shifting around and causing irritation.

Makeup hacks When you wipe down your dresser, it's a great time to wash your makeup brushes and sponges. You can wash makeup brushes in warm water with a makeup brush cleanser – simply submerge the brushes in this mixture for 15 minutes. Another hack: you can rub your brush heads against a kitchen sieve to gently help loosen any makeup. The sieve ensures every bristle is cleaned!

DEEP *clean*

Because bedrooms need frequent cleaning, they don't usually call for too much deep cleaning (yay!). The items in this section go that extra step to remove hidden allergens in your bedroom. They only need to be done every 6–12 months to make a big difference to the look and feel of your bedroom.

CHECKLIST

- ☐ Rotate and/or flip mattress
- ☐ Vacuum under bed base and behind bedhead
- ☐ Wash pillows
- ☐ Deep-clean fabric bedhead and upholstery around bedroom
- ☐ Remove mould from wardrobe, if present
- ☐ Clean air conditioner filters and ceiling fans
- ☐ Vacuum curtains, lamps, bedheads and under bed
- ☐ Rotate wardrobe, packing away seasonal items

BEDROOM DEEP CLEAN

HOW TO WASH PILLOWS

Pillows can capture sweat, skin cells and oils, so washing them every 6 months helps keep them fresh, clean and fluffy for a more refreshing night's rest.

Note: Check the care instructions on your individual pillows to make sure this process is right for you. This process is for standard synthetic blend pillows.

You'll need:

- 1 tbsp laundry detergent
- 3–4 drops eucalyptus oil (to help remove dustmites)
- Rolled-up T-shirt (tied into a ball) or 2–3 wool dryer balls (you'll find these at your local supermarket)

How to:

- Check the care instructions on your pillows. Most can be washed in the washing machine 2 at a time, with one on either side to balance the machine.
- Add laundry detergent and eucalyptus oil, then wash.
- Dry pillows flat in shade until almost dry.
- Place in the dryer for the last 10 minutes with T-shirt or wool dryer balls. This helps give the pillows that final fluff and prevents clumping.

Don't forget your quilt! This same process can also be applied to your quilt, doona or duvet every 6 months to remove stains and built-up oils.

HOW TO CLEAN YOUR FABRIC BEDHEAD

Whether you have a timber or an upholstered bedhead, they can harbour a lot of dust and dustmites. The next time you're changing your linens, give your bedhead a quick vacuum and you'll be surprised at how much dust is hiding in there.

You'll need:
- Hand vacuum
- 1 tsp dishwashing liquid
- Microfibre cloth

How to:
- Vacuum your bedhead.
- Place dishwashing liquid onto a damp microfibre cloth, then blot the stains to help lift them.

HOW TO REMOVE MOULD FROM CLOTHES AND WARDROBE

Mould can grow in wardrobes because they're damp, humid environments that often aren't adequately ventilated. The first step to removing mould is keeping the area dry – this could be through a dehumidifier or keeping your wardrobe doors open during the day to allow for airflow.

If you do find mould within your wardrobe or on your clothes, you can use the DIY mould removal spray on page 156.

PLACES EVERYONE FORGETS TO CLEAN IN THE BEDROOM

Light switches and powerpoints
These can harbour a lot of germs and bacteria. Simply wipe every month with a multipurpose spray and a microfibre cloth.

Under the bed base
What's hiding under your bed? As beds can be heavy and difficult to move, there can be a lot of dust and dirt accumulating under them – which may be scarier than the monsters you once thought lived down there! Once a year, it's a great idea to move your bed and vacuum underneath it. Use this time to flip your mattress while you're there. If you have a vacuum cleaner that reaches under your bed, you can include this area in your weekly clean to avoid the build-up.

Behind the bed
Dust piles can also form here – so to clean up hidden dust, dirt and allergens, move your bed away from the wall and give this area a quick vacuum every 6 months.

Lamps
Wipe the base of the lamp every month with a microfibre cloth and the DIY dusting spray. A simple hack to remove dust from the lamp shade is to use a clothing lint roller!

Air conditioner filters and ceiling fans

Air conditioner filters can also be a place for hidden dust and allergens to lurk, so don't forget to empty the filters and clean them frequently.

Curtains

When vacuuming your room, also run your handheld vacuum down your curtains or blinds. Some curtains can also be removed and placed in your washing machine – check the care instructions on your curtains. After vacuuming curtains and blinds, wait 10 minutes before vacuuming your floors, to leave time for the dust to settle.

Windowsills

It's also a good idea to run the vacuum across your windowsills to remove dust and dirt that may have blown inwards.

Organising

As we've seen, organising and cleaning go hand in hand, and nowhere more so than high-use places like the bedroom, so a well-organised room allows you to keep it tidy for longer. I've often lived in places that lack storage space, so I've learnt a lot of space-saving tricks that I'll be sharing throughout this section of the book. It's also important that every item within your home has a 'home'. Without designated spots for household items, mess and clutter inevitably follow. A trick I love to incorporate into my organising routine is to take 'before' and 'after' photos – it's very motivating to see how your space has been transformed, often with a few small changes!

HOW TO MAXIMISE UNDER-BED STORAGE

If you're short on space, the area under your bed can provide great hidden storage for items that are less frequently used. This could include shoes, clothes you don't regularly use, sentimental items, Christmas decorations, linens or toys in kids' bedrooms. You can find low-line, slim, large storage boxes (some even have roller wheels!) to store items airtight and make sure they stay fresh and dust-free.

If you're storing clothing, blankets or other bulky items in storage, you can also use vacuum seal bags to save further space.

HOW TO FOLD A FITTED SHEET

As tempting as it might be to roll your fitted sheet into a ball and stuff it in your linen closet, it's not the best use of space and can also leave wrinkles on your sheets. If you're low on space, this space-saving fold is for you.

- ◊ Lay your fitted sheet on a flat surface, with the elastic section facing upwards in a square shape.

- ◊ Place your hands through the bottom corners of the sheet, and place them into the top corners to form a rectangle.

- ◊ Place your hand through the left corner of the sheet and fold it into the right corner to create a small square.

- ◊ Fold the bottom and top crosswise into a thin rectangle.

- ◊ Fold the sides lengthwise. You should be left with a flat, compact square that you can store in a basket or box in your linen closet.

HOW TO FOLD LINENS INTO SETS

Once you've folded your fitted sheets, you can store them in handy bundles with the rest of your sheet sets. This simple fold keeps your sheet sets in bundles, making them quicker and easier to find in storage, while also protecting your linens from dust and allergens in storage.

- ◊ Fold your fitted sheet using the instructions above.

- ◊ Fold your flat sheet into a rectangle the same size as your fitted sheet.

- ◊ Fold your pillowcases into squares (but keep one aside).

- ◊ Turn the pillowcase you've kept aside inside out.

- ◊ Place your fitted sheet, flat sheet and pillowcases inside the pillowcase.

- ◊ Fold the pillowcase in half lengthwise, then use the flap on the pillowcase to wrap it around the bundle and secure it.

HOW TO ORGANISE YOUR DRESSER

- ◊ Take a 'before' photo of your dresser drawers – it's best to apply this method one drawer at a time.

- ◊ Start by emptying out the drawers and placing all the items in a big pile – put them in a high-use area like on your bed or in a walkway so that you're more likely to finish the task. If you'd like to do your whole dresser at once, empty all drawers into one pile to sort.

- ◊ Go through each item one by one and sort them into one pile per category: for example, sportswear, T-shirts and pants. Place the items you use more often at the top of the pile and items you use less often at the bottom.

- ◊ Meanwhile, keep a bag or box next to you and place items that you no longer use or are in need of donation directly into the box.

- ◊ Once you have your categorised piles, think about what should be near each other based on how you use the items in your wardrobe. For example, T-shirts and shorts, or underwear and socks. Fold and place the items back into the drawers accordingly.

- ◊ File folding is a great way to be able to see all items in your drawers. Instead of stacking your folded clothes into your drawers, place them vertically into your drawers so you're able to see every item when you open them.

◊ To categorise items in your drawers, you can either use bamboo drawer dividers or place your items into rows next to each other.

◊ Take your 'after' photo and use it as motivation to keep tackling declutters all around your home!

HOW TO ORGANISE SHOES

◊ Start by emptying your shoe cupboard and sorting through which shoes you wear and those you don't. Donate shoes that you don't wear anymore and store shoes you don't need at the moment (for example boots during summer, or your wedding or formal shoes).

◊ Vacuum your shoe area.

◊ Place shoes back into your wardrobe in pairs and categories like sports shoes, formal shoes and work shoes. You can place your shoes in stackable, clear shoe boxes to save space. Shelves and cubbies are also an effective way to display footwear.

HOW TO MAKE SHOES SMELL BETTER IN STORAGE
Shoes can develop odours when kept in storage, but there are some simple things you can do to stop the odours in their tracks!

◊ Place dried lavender petals into a breathable mesh bag. This can be placed inside your shoes or in the shoe cabinet.

◊ Dried coffee beans can be used to repel odours all around the home. Simply place them in a breathable mesh bag then place in your shoe cabinet.

◊ Newspaper is another great way to repel odours as it helps absorb moisture. Simply roll used newspaper into a ball and place it inside your shoes.

HOW TO MAXIMISE HANGING SPACE IN YOUR WARDROBE

◊ Start by decluttering your wardrobe and donating any items that you no longer use. Pack away seasonal items, like heavy jackets or beachwear, into storage to save space. You can do seasonal wardrobe rotations to keep your wardrobe neat – this space is often the most efficient when everything is on display.

◊ Place your items into categories based on the items – for example, jackets, T-shirts, shirts and jumpers.

◊ If you have a narrow wardrobe, you can double your wardrobe hanging space using the tabs from soda cans. Loop the tab over your hangers and use the loop to hang another hanger!

◊ Use shower curtain rings to hang handbags, scarves and belts to make sure every item has a home.

To make decluttering your wardrobe easy, turn all hangers around backwards at the beginning of the year. As you use an item, place it back in the wardrobe the correct way around, so you can easily see which items you've used and which you haven't. It's a quick way to declutter items you no longer use for donation or storage.

HOW TO ORGANISE YOUR JEWELLERY

Have you ever spent time detangling your favorite necklace while trying to rush to a party? We've all been there! Jewellery is delicate and small, so having it well organised avoids tricky tangles and damage, and helps you find what you're looking for more quickly.

◊ Invest in a jewellery box to keep your items categorised, easy to find and detangled. Jewellery boxes also help prevent dust from getting on your jewellery for pieces that you don't wear frequently. You can store your jewellery box on your dresser or on a shelf in your wardrobe to keep it safe.

◊ If you wear jewellery every day, keeping a little, shallow dish near your bedside and in your bathroom is perfect to take your items off and keep them safe until you're ready to use them again.

◊ If you own a lot of necklaces that are at risk of getting tangled, using a stick-on hook on the back of your door or side of your cupboard can save you time detangling later.

◊ Mini magnetic pads can be useful to keep earrings on so they don't roll away or get misplaced.

HOW TO ORGANISE JEANS

Jeans can take up quite a bit of room in your wardrobe. Whether your wardrobe has more shelf space or more hanging space, you can use either option to store and organise your jeans.

How to fold jeans for shelf storage:

- ◊ Place your jeans on a bed or flat surface.

- ◊ Fold them in half crosswise.

- ◊ Fold them lengthways into thirds from the bottom up.

- ◊ Place on your shelves.

How to hang jeans for wardrobe storage:

- ◊ Place your jeans on a bed or flat surface.

- ◊ Fold them in half crosswise.

- ◊ Loop a belt buckle around the top of a hanger.

- ◊ Fold the bottom of the jeans and loop it onto the bar of the hanger.

- ◊ Hang within your wardrobe.

ORGANISING TIPS FOR *kids' bedrooms*

Kids' bedrooms can be a mess – between toys, clothes, shoes, homework, pens and pencils, they're usually a dumping ground. Involving your children in the process and giving them responsibility for their space is a great way to keep this area under control. Gamifying bedroom cleaning is one of the best ways to get them excited about cleaning their space. Try setting a countdown timer and see who can clean the quickest, or play a fun song to bring some joy and excitement to the process.

TOYS

Decluttering toys can seem like a never-ending process. Keeping them in tubs and organisers will make sure everything has a 'home'. Tubs can be labelled with pictures so that even kids who aren't able to read yet can see which tubs are for building blocks, cars, dolls or train sets.

> Many soft toys can be washed in the washing machine to prevent dustmites and allergens forming on them. Check the care instructions on your children's plush toys and wash them every few months to keep them fresh and clean.

TOY ROTATIONS

These are a great way to limit the amount of toys that kids have at any given time, reducing mess and clutter. Instead of having all the toys out at once, you can break them up into smaller groups and pull out new groups of toys every month in order to put the other ones in storage. This helps kids keep interest in their toys, avoids overstimulation and helps save money on buying excessive amounts of toys. A win-win!

> Many plastic toys (non-battery-operated) can be washed in a solution of mild soapy water. Legos are a great example of plastic toys that can harbour a lot of dirt, so soaking them every few months helps keep the play area clean and germ-free.

WARDROBES

Children's wardrobes can be difficult to organise, especially if your kids like choosing their own outfits like mine do. Keeping items folded and in their proper spot can be a challenging task, but there are a few simple tips and tricks to make the job easier.

File folding

As with the tips for your own wardrobe, folding for vertical storage allows you to see all the clothes you have at a snapshot. This can allow kids to assert their independence – they can pick their own outfits without pulling everything out to make a decision.

Uniforms

I find it a lot easier to store them on hangers to cut down on ironing. Simply pull them straight from the washing machine or dryer, then hang them on a hanger and allow them to air-dry without wrinkles forming.

Outgrown clothes

If you love to hold on to your kids' outgrown clothes, or perhaps you're keeping them for a future child, vacuum seal bags can be a great solution to keep them dust-free, airtight and space-saved. Vacuum-seal the clothes, place them into a clear, slim-line roller tub, then slide them under beds until you need them again.

Clothes that are too big

On the flipside, many people (myself included) often have clothes that their kids don't quite fit into yet. They may be gifts or purchases for the future. I also like to keep these items stored in vacuum seal bags, but instead of placing them under the bed where it's difficult to see, place them above the cupboard in a clear container, so you're aware of what you have.

Bonus tip Take a photo of the clothes your kids have. You can refer to this on the go when you're looking to buy the next item. This can save you from purchasing duplicates and help save you money as well.

PAPERWORK AND ARTS AND CRAFTS

Arts and craft supplies can quickly take over your kids' bedrooms! To keep them organised, you can use a cart to store arts, crafts and supplies. Opt for a cart with around 3–4 shelves so there's enough storage, and preferably one with wheels so you can move it around easily. Make sure to leave 1–2 shelves empty so there's room if more supplies are purchased.

When it comes to labelling your cart, use chalkboard or washable labels. As the items frequently change, the labels can be updated quickly and easily.

To organise artwork once it's been created, a file folio can be helpful to keep key pieces. You can add stickers and labels to the folio pages to keep track of children's ages to look back on their masterpieces! You can also keep a separate folio for key pieces of kids' schoolwork.

ORGANISING TIPS FOR *guest bedrooms*

For those lucky enough to have guest bedrooms, unless you have a lot of guests stay over, these rooms are often unused for much of the year. There are some simple ways to make the most of them as an important storage space without cluttering the area.

TALLBOYS

These can be used to store seasonal items like sweaters, thermals or beach gear, and extra sets of linens. This also allows your guests to have a spare change of linen should they need it during their stay.

WARDROBES

You can use the space in your guest bedroom wardrobe for hanging seasonal items, like coats, suits and formal dresses. Make sure these are easy to remove when needed, and always keep enough room for a suitcase or two in the wardrobe for unexpected visitors.

BEDSIDES

It's best to leave guest bedsides empty as they can be difficult to empty before guests arrive. You can store extra books or magazines in the drawers.

UNDER-BED STORAGE

As with the other rooms, don't overlook under-bed storage for items you rarely use, like Christmas and Halloween decorations.

Styling

As I said at the beginning of this chapter, the way your bedroom is styled can transform it from a place of practicality to one of rest and relaxation, improving the quality of your sleep and the outlook of your day.

Imagine waking up in the morning and starting your day in soft sheets, turning around to look at your beautiful, clutter-free bedsides and waking to a clean, organised space. Your bedroom doesn't need to be perfectly styled like a magazine, but it's small changes like these that can allow you to create the right space for you to start and finish your day in.

HOW TO CLEAN AND STYLE YOUR BED

◊ Strip your bed of all linens and use a handheld vacuum to vacuum your mattress and headboard to remove dust and allergens.

◊ Place a mattress protector or mattress topper on to protect your mattress against stains and spills.

◊ Place a fitted sheet over your mattress protector.

◊ Place a flat sheet over your fitted sheet. By using a flat sheet you can reduce the frequency you wash your quilt cover, as it acts as a barrier between you and your quilt. You can spray linen spray or a light mist of tap water on your flat sheet as you tuck it in to remove any wrinkles without ironing.

◊ Place your quilt on your bed and roll it one-third of the way down your bed and back up, to roll the top into an S shape.

◊ Place a blanket underneath this roll to add height and make your bed look fluffier.

◊ Place pillows on your bed. How many pillows you use is up to you, but I use 2 European pillows at the back (60 cm x 60 cm) followed by 4 standard cushions in the front for a double or queen-sized bed. For a king-sized bed, I recommend 3 European pillows at the back and 4 king-sized pillows stacked in the front.

◊ Finish with a feature cushion and a calming linen spray for an impressive bedding look.

Tip Keep pillows looking and feeling fluffy by placing them in the dryer with a tennis ball wrapped in a sock for 5 minutes before placing them on your bed.

HOW TO FOLD HOSPITAL CORNERS

This is a free way to add some simple luxury to your bedroom. Treat yourself to this fold the next time you make your bed to bring the hotel experience home.

◊ Lay your sheet across the bed and tuck in the base of the sheet only.

◊ Lift the side into a triangle and place on the mattress.

◊ Tuck in the base of the triangle.

◊ Tuck the triangle into the base of the bed.

HOW TO STYLE YOUR BEDSIDES

There are a few ways to keep your bedsides organised, uncluttered and practical, so you have what you need overnight but can wake up to a clear space.

◊ **Use the rule of thirds:** The rule of thirds states that items arranged in groupings of odd numbers are more visually appealing than even-numbered groupings. On your bedside, this could mean creating a triangular shape with three styling items, like a vase, candle and dish. To further reduce visual clutter on your bedside, try grouping beautiful décor items together on a tray then keep your practical items next to it.

◊ **Stick-on hooks to say goodbye to wires:** If you do keep your phone by your bedside, you can hide unsightly wires using stick-on hooks. Simply place 1–2 hooks on the side of your bedside and loop your phone charger on it to prevent wires ending up on the floor.

◊ **Drink bottles:** Choose a drink bottle in a colour or pattern that matches your bedroom aesthetic. You could even switch out your drink bottle for a glass jug and fluted glass to bring that simple luxury into your bedroom.

◊ **Candle for aroma:** Don't underestimate the power of smell! Hotels often use the techniques of 'scent marketing' to bring guests into a full sensory experience, and it's easy to achieve the same effect in your bedroom.

Bedroom routines and checklists

- ☐ Make bed
- ☐ Clear cups and other clutter from bedsides
- ☐ Put away clothes in wardrobe
- ☐ Place dirty clothes in laundry basket
- ☐ Keep outfits ready and bags packed for next morning
- ☐ Change and wash pillowcase every 3–4 days

DAILY BEDROOM CLEAN

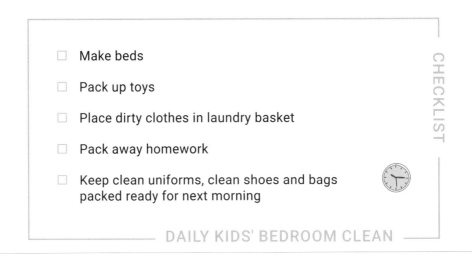

CHECKLIST

- ☐ Make beds
- ☐ Pack up toys
- ☐ Place dirty clothes in laundry basket
- ☐ Pack away homework
- ☐ Keep clean uniforms, clean shoes and bags packed ready for next morning

DAILY KIDS' BEDROOM CLEAN

THE DREAM CLEAN

CHECKLIST

WEEKLY BEDROOM CLEAN

- ☐ Remove sheets
- ☐ Air mattress
- ☐ Vacuum mattress
- ☐ Add new sheets
- ☐ Wipe down bedside tables
- ☐ Vacuum floors
- ☐ Wipe down mirrors (see page 153 for the DIY window cleaner spray)
- ☐ Wipe down dresser and clean makeup brushes

CHECKLIST

MONTHLY BEDROOM CLEAN

- ☐ Vacuum curtains
- ☐ Vacuum windowsills
- ☐ Deodorise mattress
- ☐ Spot-clean fabric bedhead
- ☐ Move bedside tables and vacuum behind them
- ☐ Wash throws
- ☐ Wipe down light switches
- ☐ Wipe down lamps

CHECKLIST

BEDROOM DEEP CLEAN

- ☐ Rotate and/or flip mattress
- ☐ Vacuum under bed base and behind bedhead
- ☐ Wash pillows
- ☐ Deep-clean fabric bedhead and upholstery around bedroom
- ☐ Remove mould from wardrobe, if present
- ☐ Clean air conditioner filters and ceiling fans
- ☐ Vacuum curtains, lamps, bedheads and under bed
- ☐ Rotate wardrobe, packing away seasonal items

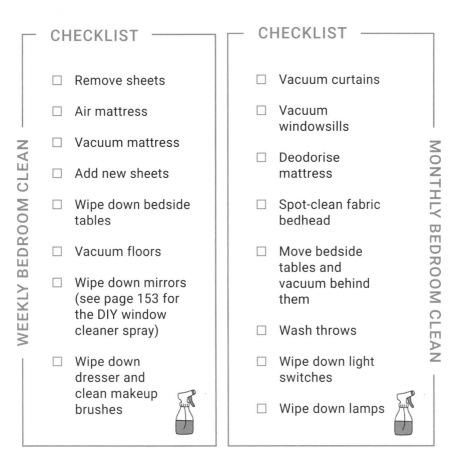

CHAPTER 4

Bathroom

When your bathroom is clean and organised, it can be one of the most tranquil spaces in your home, a sanctuary away from the hustle and bustle. Think about your favourite spa or favourite retreat – what was it that made you feel calm? It might have been the softened towels, the fresh smell of eucalyptus, the calming music or even simply the shining, clutter-free space. You can create that same feeling in your own home to come back to every day – and all it takes is a few simple steps.

Because bathrooms see a lot of daily use, and we really get up close and personal with them, they're one of the areas around the home that can get the dirtiest the fastest – and they're the room most likely to be seen by visitors! Bathrooms can also build up mildew and mould quickly, so ensuring the area is kept dry and clean is the best way to avoid grime.

Many store-bought bathroom cleaners contain heavy-duty and harsh chemicals that can fill your home with fumes. The DIYs you'll find in this chapter are lower-tox and eco-friendly alternatives to these cleaners; many of the DIYs can be made in bulk and be kept for up to 3 months.

As with kitchens, bathrooms are used by all household members, so they're another great place to share the workload. If you have multiple bathrooms, each person could be responsible for cleaning their own space. If you have one or two shared bathrooms, you could share the workload on a rotating roster. You can get younger kids involved by encouraging them to pick up their own bath toys and put them away, or by asking them to put their toothbrushes in the cupboard after use, instead of leaving them on the vanity. It's all the small things that will ultimately make a big difference.

Bathroom cleaning can seem daunting, but it only takes about 15 minutes to complete a quick clean. Pop on a playlist and use the echo of your bathroom to make cleaning fun! Play your favourite power ballad and use the reverb to create your own mini concert hall.

As bathroom cleaning doesn't have a one-size-fits-all approach, you can start this chapter with whatever cleaning routine works best for you. If you're looking for ways to make bathroom cleaning more manageable, start at Clean in 15 to build those routines into your week. If your bathroom has been a bit neglected and needs some initial TLC (we've all been there!), start at the Deep Clean section.

CLEANING *playlist*

Clean in 15

A weekly 15-minute clean can make a huge difference to your bathroom. This is the space where you can notice a quick clean the most, as you make those tiles and chrome fixtures shine and restore a fresh smell. It goes deeper than surface level though – keeping on top of a clean bathroom space helps you to remove bacteria and germs that cause illness and eliminate dust and grime from surfaces.

Our starting point for a 15-minute clean is to remove towels and bathmats, then spray your bathroom – especially the shower, bathtub and vanity – with the multipurpose spray. Leave it for 10 minutes while you clean the toilet. Then, when you wipe down everything, there shouldn't be much heavy scrubbing needed. Finally, empty your bin and add in fresh bath towels.

How you clean your bathroom will differ based on your household structure and how many people are using your bathroom. The checklists in this section are a guide, and the weekly bathroom clean can be used on a rotating roster to share the load with all members of the household.

The bathroom can be the most satisfying room to clean – it's very little effort for maximum reward!

Fits like a glove

As a rule of thumb, when cleaning the bathroom it's important to wear gloves to protect yourself from bacteria and illnesses. Although the DIYs in this chapter involve gentler cleaning products that are unlikely to cause skin irritations, like many commercial products can, it's always a good idea to wear gloves to protect yourself. Keep your bathroom gloves in a separate section of your cleaning caddy, away from your kitchen gloves!

CHECKLIST

- ☐ Clean shower
- ☐ Empty kids' toys from bathtub
- ☐ Clean bathtub
- ☐ Clean toilet
- ☐ Clean toilet paper holder
- ☐ Wipe sink and cabinets
- ☐ Clean mirrors
- ☐ Check which items require restock and write on shopping list
- ☐ Wash and replace towels and bathmat
- ☐ Wipe down doorknobs, light switches and light fixtures
- ☐ Vacuum and mop floors using the DIY floor cleaner (page 41)
- ☐ Empty bin

DIY Multipurpose Bathroom Spray

This spray is an all-rounder that takes the dirty work and elbow grease out of cleaning your bathroom. It can be used on showers, shower screens, bathtubs, vanities and tiles to leave them clean and sparkling. The acidity in the white vinegar helps dissolve bathroom dirt and grime, while the tea-tree oil is a natural antifungal to help keep mould away for longer.

You'll need:

- Spray bottle
- 1 cup white vinegar
- 1 cup water
- 2 tbsp dishwashing liquid
- 4 drops tea-tree oil

Tip

Substitute tea-tree oil with clove oil in this mixture for an extra mould preventative!

How to:

- In your spray bottle, combine white vinegar, water, dishwashing liquid and tea-tree oil.
- Spray around your bathroom, then leave for 10 minutes.
- Simply wipe and rinse! Make sure the shower is rinsed afterwards to ensure there is no soap residue left.

White vinegar is not suitable for all bathroom surfaces. If you have a marble or natural stone bathroom, try this mix instead:

- ◊ 1 cup water
- ◊ 2 tsp castile soap
- ◊ 4 drops tea-tree oil

To save even more time, add this mix into a dishwashing brush! These are scrubbing tools with a scratch-resistant sponge at the end, and a tube that dispenses the product as you scrub – they remove the need to spray and wipe separately, as it's being done at the same time.

DIY Fizzing Toilet-Cleaning Bombs

These are an easy way to clean your toilet without harsh chemicals, while also leaving your whole bathroom smelling fresh! The bombs can be used on your weekly bathroom clean, or as needed as a refresher when guests come over. You can make them in advance (monthly or quarterly) – simply store them airtight and use them as needed.

You'll need:

- Bowl
- 1 cup baking soda
- ¼ cup citric acid (You'll find this in the baking aisle of your supermarket)
- 10 drops lemon essential oil
- Water or 3% hydrogen peroxide in a spray bottle
- Silicone dome moulds (You'll find these at your local cake-decorating store or online)
- Airtight jar

How to:

- In a bowl, mix baking soda, citric acid and essential oil.
- Spray this mixture with hydrogen peroxide or tap water until the mixture forms a consistency similar to wet sand.
- Press into the silicone mould and allow to set overnight.
- Once set, remove from moulds and place in an airtight jar out of reach from pets or children.
- To use, place one toilet-cleaner bomb in your toilet and allow to fizz for 10 minutes. Then simply scrub and flush!

Tip After cleaning the toilet, you can dry the brush by placing it under the toilet seat. This way it dries over the toilet bowl, allowing your holders to remain clean.

DIY Magic Mirror Cleaner

Mirror, mirror on the wall, what's the best cleaning product of them all? This DIY mirror cleaner! This spray can be used for mirrors all around your home to keep them shiny and streak-free, removing all those pesky stains – sunscreen, toothpaste and moisturiser, for example – that build up over time. In this DIY, the white vinegar and water help mirrors shine and the isopropyl / rubbing alcohol makes it dry very fast, which helps avoid streaks. This method should be applied with your weekly bathroom clean.

You'll need:

- ¼ cup water
- ¼ cup white vinegar
- ¼ cup isopropyl / rubbing alcohol
- 10 drops lemon essential oil
- Spray bottle

How to:

- Mix water, white vinegar, rubbing alcohol and essential oil in a spray bottle.
- Shake and use as required.

I love using lemon essential oil in this DIY, but as it is for fragrance only, you can use whichever essential oil you like.

THE MAGIC OF SHAVING CREAM

There's a product that you likely already have sitting in your bathroom vanity which is wonderful at keeping your bathroom mirrors cleaner for longer. Simply apply a small pump of shaving cream to a microfibre cloth (a little goes a long way!), then buff into your mirrors until the mixture becomes transparent. Keep buffing with a dry microfibre cloth until your mirrors are fully clear. Shaving cream helps keep fingerprint marks away for longer and prevents mirrors from fogging up with steam – it works a treat.

QUICK TIPS AND TRICKS TO MAKE YOUR BATHROOM SMELL *amazing*

◊ Fill a jar with ¼ cup uncooked rice and a few drops of essential oil. Place this in your bathroom to help absorb unwanted moisture and keep the area fresh.

◊ Hang a bunch of eucalyptus leaves in the shower under your shower head. When the shower is running, the steam helps release the eucalyptus oil, which smells amazing and gives your bathroom a spa-like feeling.

◊ Add 2–3 drops of essential oils onto cotton balls. Hide these balls around your bathroom (inside a vase is perfect!) to add hidden fragrance and keep it smelling fresh and clean.

PLACES EVERYONE FORGETS TO CLEAN IN THE BATHROOM

There can be so many hidden nooks and crannies in your bathroom where dirt and grime lurk! Some of the most frequently overlooked places are also often the easiest to clean. Here are some places you may be missing.

Bathmats

These can be the culprit behind musty bathroom odours, but it is possible to remove that musty smell and make them feel and smell brand new. Add 5–10 drops of essential oil (I like using peppermint) into ½ cup baking soda – this works together to deodorise. Sprinkle the mixture over your bathmat and leave for 15 minutes, then place the mat in your washing machine and wash with your normal laundry detergent.

The sink overflow

Have you noticed that little hole at the back of your sink that sometimes has a little silver cap over it? That is your sink overflow. All sorts of gunk can build up in there, so simply scrub clean with an old toothbrush every 6 months or so.

Shower curtains

These are magnets for mould and mildew, but you don't need to replace them when they're looking worse for wear. Simply place your shower curtain in the washing machine with a few towels (towels help soften the agitation of the spin cycle) and wash on a cold cycle with liquid detergent. They should come out looking brand new!

The toilet paper holder
Due to its proximity to – you guessed it, the toilet – the very overlooked toilet holder may need a bit of TLC. Simply wipe it down with the DIY multipurpose spray weekly when you're cleaning the rest of the bathroom.

Light fixtures
Bathroom light fixtures and heat lamps can build up a lot of dust and dirt due to the damp environment. Simply give these a quick wipe with a damp microfibre cloth during your next bathroom clean.

Doorknobs and light switches
These are often overlooked too, so make sure to give these a quick wipe down when needed.

The toothbrush holder
When was the last time you looked inside your toothbrush holder? It can be harbouring bacteria, germs and pools of stagnant water. Simply place into your dishwasher every month to keep it clean and fresh.

CLEAN IT *like you mean it*

On a monthly or quarterly basis, it's good to give a little bit of extra TLC to our bathrooms, to maintain proper hygiene and keep the space shining. This deeper clean is the perfect time to pop on a great playlist or podcast, get the family involved and add those extra tasks to your routine. You'll feel so much better once they're done!

CHECKLIST

- ☐ Clean grout
- ☐ Clean wall tiles
- ☐ Polish fixtures
- ☐ Clean bathtubs
- ☐ Clean showers
- ☐ Remove limescale from your shower screens
- ☐ Wipe windowsills and windows
- ☐ Clean bin
- ☐ Place the toothbrush holder in the dishwasher (you'll be surprised at how dirty it can get!)

HOW TO CLEAN GROUT

Grout cleaning is not a glamorous task, but this simple mix makes the process a lot quicker and easier. The 3% hydrogen peroxide helps whiten and brighten grout, and the baking soda is a natural abrasive to make scrubbing much easier. You can also invest in a telescopic power scrubber to make this task less demanding on your back.

You'll need:
- 1 cup baking soda
- ⅓ cup 3% hydrogen peroxide
- 1 tsp dishwashing liquid
- 1 tsp water
- Grout brush or power scrubber
- Mop

How to:
- In a bowl, mix baking soda, hydrogen peroxide, dishwashing liquid and water until you get a smooth paste consistency. If the mixture is too runny, add more baking soda. If it's too firm, add a dash of water.
- Apply paste to your grout using a grout brush or power scrubber and leave on for 15 minutes. Make sure pets and children avoid the area during this time.
- Scrub the grout with a grout brush or power scrubber and mop up any excess mixture off the floor.

HOW TO CLEAN BATHROOM WALL TILES

A flat microfibre mop can make cleaning your wall tiles easy! Some microfibre mops also have a built-in spray compartment which you can add your cleaning mix to. Simply use the microfibre mop to wipe grime and dirt off the walls with ease.

HOW TO POLISH CHROME FIXTURES

Keeping chrome fixtures clean is easier than you may think! All you need is some white vinegar – it's your best friend at cleaning and removing limescale and polishing chrome fixtures like showerheads and taps.

You'll need:

- Microfibre cloth
- White vinegar

How to:

- Soak a microfibre cloth in white vinegar.
- Wrap around your chrome fixtures and leave for 10 minutes.
- Rinse to reveal polished chrome fixtures.

This method is only suitable for chrome fixtures. If you have black, gold or any coated fixtures, simply use a small amount of gentle dishwashing liquid on a microfibre cloth to clean them. This will preserve the coating.

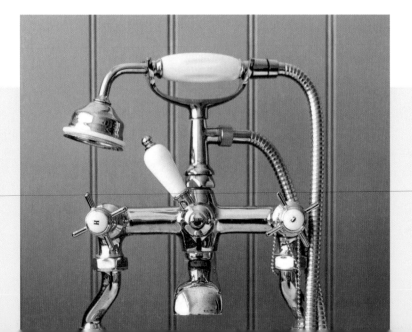

DIY Magic Bathtub Cleaner

The multipurpose spray works wonderfully on weekly bathtub cleans, but this DIY is perfect when you need to give your bathtub a deep clean. It may not need to be used every bathroom clean, but it's tough on pesky bathtub rings when they appear.

You'll need:

- Microwave-proof jug
- ½ cup white vinegar
- ½ cup dishwashing liquid
- Cloth

How to:

- In a microwave-proof jug, heat white vinegar in the microwave for a few seconds until warm.
- Add dishwashing liquid and stir.
- Pour this mixture over your bathtub and spread so it covers all dirty areas.
- Leave on for 15–20 minutes while the mixture does the hard work of removing soap scum and dirt.
- Wipe and rinse.

◊ Remove all containers and accessories from the shower.

◊ Spray multipurpose bathroom spray (see page 142) across the entire shower and leave for 10 minutes.

◊ If you have a shower curtain, remove it and put it in the washing machine (following the steps on page 147).

◊ If you have a glass shower screen, use the DIY glass cleaner (see page 153) to remove any limescale or build-up, then clean with a microfibre cloth.

◊ If you have any mould on your ceiling, use the DIY mould spray (see page 156) to clean the mould.

◊ Scrub the shower with a bristle brush or a power scrubber to remove grime and build-up.

◊ Rinse the entire shower with hot water before restocking.

DIY Magic Glass Cleaner

This magic glass cleaner is amazing at leaving any glass around your home looking clean and spotless. You can use it on shower screens, windows, pool fences or any glass around your home.

You'll need:

- Spray bottle
- 1 cup white vinegar
- ½ cup dishwashing liquid
- 1 cup water
- Squeegee

How to:

- In a spray bottle, mix white vinegar, dishwashing liquid and water.
- Spray on glass and wipe with a squeegee.
- Rinse by washing with water, or with a squeegee and a bucket of water.

If using this mix on your windows, you can use a 50/50 mix of white vinegar and water to leave the internal side of your windows shining. Wipe this mixture with a lint-free cloth or microfibre cloth.

Tip To keep your windows shining for longer, try using a water repellent after cleaning them. You can find these at your local hardware stores or automotive stores, as they're usually used for car windscreens – but they also work great on shower screens or external windows.

HOW TO CLEAN WINDOWSILLS

Windowsills and internal windows of your bathroom are prone to build-up of mould and dirt. A quick wipe with the multipurpose spray once a month is a great way to keep dirt and mould away from this area. You can use an old toothbrush to reach any tight corners.

To clean the tricky window tracks around window opening, don't forget this simple trick from chapter 2! Lay a flat sponge on your window railing and note with a marker where the tracks are. Using scissors, gently slice the sponge lengthways where the tracks would sit, but not cutting all the way through. This sponge will now clean your window or door tracks easily.

HOW TO CLEAN YOUR BATHROOM BIN

Bathroom bins should be cleaned every 2 weeks to remove germs, bacteria and any odours. Wipe the empty bin with the multipurpose bathroom spray, then rinse with hot water.

Tip Keep washing all bins around the home on the same fortnightly rotation, so you can do them all at the same time!

Tip To soak up bin spills, line the bottom of your bin liner with old newspaper. This will help absorb any spills or liquid so that your bins remain dry.

Tip To keep your bins smelling fresher for longer, add 4–6 drops of an essential oil of your choice on 2–3 cotton balls. Place these under your bin liner to add hidden fragrance to your bin.

Deep *clean*

As with our quick and intermediate cleans, a deep clean allows you to disinfect those areas that are otherwise often overlooked and make sure your bathroom is a clean, germ-free space. By dedicating some time towards deep cleaning, you can also cover off those hard-to-reach spots to save you time and money in the future. For example, cleaning your bathroom exhaust annually can help it run more efficiently and help you save money on your power bills – a win-win!

CHECKLIST

- ☐ Remove mould from your bathroom
- ☐ Clean under toilet seats
- ☐ Deodorise drains
- ☐ Wipe down bathroom fans and ventilators, and clean filters
- ☐ Deep-clean showerhead
- ☐ Clean bathroom cleaning tools

BATHROOM DEEP CLEAN

DIY Mould Removal Spray

This will become your go-to. Not only does it help remove mould from the surface, the mix of tea-tree and clove oils provides 2 natural antifungals and antibacterials to help remove mould spores.

Note: This is only for smaller amounts of mould – always consult a professional if you have a large build-up of mould in your home.

You'll need:
- Spray bottle
- 1 cup white vinegar
- 20 drops tea-tree oil
- 20 drops clove oil
- Cloth

How to:
- In a spray bottle, mix white vinegar, tea-tree oil and clove oil.
- Spray on affected areas and wait 20 minutes, then wipe and rinse the mixture away.

Tip Mould grows in damp environments, so try to keep your bathroom well ventilated to avoid it building up, either with an exhaust fan or by opening a window.

WHAT IS MOULD AND WHY DOES IT OCCUR?

Mould is a type of fungus that grows within damp and poorly ventilated areas, such as leaking roofs, leaking windows, bathrooms and ceilings. Mould reproduces by making tiny particles called spores. As spores are microscopic, they can be carried through the air and cause health problems when inhaled, including skin and eye irritation, breathing difficulties or wheezing. That's why it's important to remove mould as soon as you see it forming, and to always wear gloves and a mask when cleaning it.

If you have large amounts of mould within your home, it's always best to consult a professional for removal. For smaller amounts, the DIY spray helps remove mould from surfaces by killing the spores. Clove oil is a powerful ingredient in this DIY as it helps to kill mould spores, instead of just bleaching them. This spray can be used all around the home, in bathrooms, wardrobes and even clothes.

When removing mould from your home, it's important to address the root cause to prevent it from returning. You can do this by wiping away condensation, improving ventilation, adding appropriate drainage, fixing home leaks, opening windows and/or by using a dehumidifier to reduce humidity.

HOW TO AVOID RUST IN THE BATHROOM

Bathrooms can also be particularly prone to rust, and there are some simple ways to avoid this build-up:

◊ Before placing cans in your bathroom, place clear nail polish on the base and allow it to dry. This helps coat the metal and prevents rust rings.

◊ White vinegar is great at removing rust stains. The DIY multipurpose bathroom spray contains a large amount of vinegar to help keep rust at bay.

◊ A key part of preventing rust in water-based environments like bathrooms is making sure areas are dry. Bathroom exhaust and ventilation is one way, as is wiping down bathroom fixtures regularly with towels and cloths.

HOW TO CLEAN UNDER YOUR TOILET SEAT

When was the last time you removed your toilet seat and deep-cleaned under it? Most new toilet seats have a silver button under the seat – simply press this and the entire toilet seat will come off! This makes it so easy to clean those hidden nooks and crannies that otherwise can get overlooked.

DIY Drain Cleaner

Bathroom smelling musty? Your drains could be the cause. Lurking down the drain there may be a build-up of soap scum, hair and other nasty bacterias. The great news is that it's very easy to clean and deodorise this area, and it uses two items you probably have in your pantry right now.

You'll need:

- ½ cup baking soda
- ½ cup white vinegar

How to:

- Pour baking soda down your drain, then follow by right away pouring in white vinegar.
- The reaction will be immediate, as the mixture bubbles to remove any stuck debris.
- Leave for 10 minutes, then flush with warm water. Repeat the process if required.

THE DREAM CLEAN

HOW TO CLEAN YOUR SHOWERHEAD

The tiny holes in showerheads that water passes through daily can get blocked with mineral deposits. Keep your water pressure stronger and your shower head flowing freely with this simple trick:

◊ Fill a sandwich bag halfway with white vinegar.

◊ Place your showerhead inside the bag and submerge it within the white vinegar, then tie up the bag.

◊ Let it sit for 30 minutes.

◊ Remove the bag and rinse the showerhead with water. This process should leave your shower head sparkling clean – but be warned, when you try this for the first time, you might be shocked by the gunk that comes out!

Note: This trick works well on chrome showerheads only. For brass or black showerheads, simply wipe the showerhead with a gentle dishwashing detergent and a microfibre cloth to avoid damaging the finish.

HOW TO CLEAN YOUR BATHROOM CLEANING TOOLS

◊ Toilet brushes: These are often a breeding ground for bacteria! The easiest way to clean them is to wash the brush after each use. Simply place the brush over your toilet, held in place under the toilet seat, then spray it with multipurpose spray and pour boiling water over. Allow it to drip-dry over your toilet before placing it back into the holder.

◊ Mop heads: Many mop heads can simply be washed in a separate load in the washing machine with liquid detergent.

- ◊ **Microfibre cloths:** Machine-wash these using a mild detergent, without fabric softener as this can clog the microfibre. You'll also want to avoid heat when drying as this can damage the microfibre; instead, just dry flat in the shade. Microfibre cloths dry relatively quickly, which is why they're perfect for cleaning all around the home.

- ◊ **Gloves:** These can be washed exactly like how you'd wash your hands – just lather them up with soap and give them a thorough clean!

Organising

Bathroom cabinets and drawers contain a lot of small items, from skincare products and toothpastes to haircare and even cleaning products. Simple categorisation and organisation goes a long way in this space to make sure you can always find what you're looking for.

UNDER-VANITY *organisation*

- ◊ Start by clearing the area. Pull all items out and dispose of or donate any items that you no longer need.

- ◊ Once you've decluttered, place your items into categories: for example, haircare, skincare, cleaning, backstock.

- ◊ Clear, stackable, pull-out containers are perfect for this area, to maximise space and see exactly which items you have. Place your categorised items into these containers, and you can even label them to take your organisation to the next level.

◊ If you have multiple members of the household using this area, another alternative is to label a box for each person to separate their belongings.

A trick to buy the right-sized containers for your space is to line the bottom of your drawers with baking paper, or a large piece of scrap paper. Trace the size of your drawer and cut it out. Carry that piece of paper with you to the shops and you can lay your organisers on the paper to measure and visualise how the organisers would fit.

BATHROOM DRAWERS

Bathroom drawers can be organised based on different needs: one for haircare, skincare and makeup, one for toothbrushes and a less accessible one for towels. Think about how often you use the products, and put the items you use most frequently in the top drawers, like toothbrushes and skincare, and the less used items at the bottom, like towels, backstock or toilet roll.

SHOWER STORAGE

Start by decluttering, only leaving items in the shower that you use on a daily basis. You can either use a shower caddy or your shower niche to display your products. If you still find the shower space to be too visually cluttered, you can buy matching 4L pump bottles and dispense your product into them to make the space look more refined and spa-like.

BATH TOYS

These can take up a lot of space in the bathroom and can grow mould inside them if they are left stagnant in the bath. One solution is to buy slim organisers to slot in next to your bathtub, in order to organise bath toys and keep them accessible when needed. You can also use these slim organisers to hold bath bombs and bath accessories.

Styling

Once your bathroom is clean and organised, now comes the fun part! Taking some steps to style your bathroom can change it from a place of function to a place of retreat. Though cleaning the grime and dirt away from your bathroom will make the space feel better, there are simple ways you can take the cleaning experience to the next level and make it a truly pleasant space to relax in.

You don't need to spend much to create this feeling in your own home. It could be as simple as adding some low lighting like candles to the space, rolling your towels, or adding a touch of personality with some artwork or greenery. This is a subtle mindset shift in how to perceive the space – starting to see the bathroom as a luxury hotel experience where you can unwind after a long day.

QUICK BATHROOM STYLING TIPS

Here are some inexpensive tips that can help you turn your bathroom into your own mini-haven:

◊ Make washing your hands a spa-like experience: Investing in a great-smelling handwash and matching hand cream will add a touch of luxury to your bathroom.

◊ Make mini vignettes with 3–4 styling items: Vignettes are a grouping of décor items, like clusters of candles, flowers and towels, and you can use these to brighten up your bathroom. You can also display small jars in a cluster and fill them with cotton balls or cotton buds for a practical and beautiful storage solution.

◊ Make your toilet paper look fancier: Simply fold the end of the toilet paper into a triangle, and create a DIY seal by pressing it against the base of your tap. This is a finish you'll see in many luxury hotels.

◊ How to roll your towels like a spa does: Spa-rolling towels is a great way to add décor to your bathroom in a way that is cost-effective, functional and elegant.

- Lay your towel down horizontally on a flat surface.
- Fold one top corner down to create a triangle shape, then fold the towel in half.
- Flip the entire towel around, so the folds are underneath.
- Starting at the flat side, roll the towel towards the pointy side.
- Tuck the end into the side of the roll.

Bathroom routines and checklists

CHECKLIST

- ☐ Clean shower
- ☐ Empty kids' toys from bathtub
- ☐ Clean bathtub
- ☐ Clean toilet
- ☐ Clean toilet paper holder
- ☐ Wipe sink and cabinets
- ☐ Clean mirrors
- ☐ Check which items require restock and write on shopping list
- ☐ Wash and replace towels and bathmat
- ☐ Wipe down doorknobs, light switches and light fixtures
- ☐ Vacuum and mop floors using the DIY floor cleaner (page 41)
- ☐ Empty bin

CHECKLIST

- ☐ Clean grout
- ☐ Clean wall tiles
- ☐ Polish fixtures
- ☐ Clean bathtubs
- ☐ Clean showers
- ☐ Remove limescale from your shower screens
- ☐ Wipe windowsills and windows
- ☐ Clean bin
- ☐ Place the toothbrush holder in the dishwasher (you'll be surprised at how dirty it can get!)

CHECKLIST

- ☐ Remove mould from your bathroom
- ☐ Clean under toilet seats
- ☐ Deodorise drains
- ☐ Wipe down bathroom fans and ventilators, and clean filters
- ☐ Deep-clean showerhead
- ☐ Clean bathroom cleaning tools

BATHROOM DEEP CLEAN

CHAPTER 5

Laundry

Laundry can be a never-ending story! Stains, spills, sweat and dirt can build up daily, so it's rare to see your washing pile completely empty and tidy. And because the laundry is the room where more heavy-duty cleaning takes place, it's all the more important to keep it in good shape to maintain the overall hygiene of the household.

After a long week, the last thing you want to do is tackle a large pile of laundry or a messy laundry room. **I find the best way to approach laundry is by doing a little bit each day.** For a larger household it may mean one load per day, and for other households it may mean a load every few days or even once a week. It can take a little while to get used to the idea of doing more frequent laundry, but once you get into the swing of it, it makes a big difference to feeling less overwhelmed by the prospect.

They say it takes 30 days to build a habit, so start by setting yourself a goal of doing washing more regularly for one month. If it works for you and your household (I'm betting it will!), then it will be easier to juggle as it will become part of your routine.

Many washing machines have a 'delay start' function, which can be a game-changer. This function allows you to load your washing machine, and it will turn on automatically at the time you set. For example, you could load your washing machine before you go to bed, then set it to turn on early in the morning so you wake up with your clothes freshly washed and ready for drying. Or you could set it to start during your drive home from work, so the clothes are freshly washed and ready for drying when you get home.

This is probably an unpopular opinion, but I actually really enjoy doing laundry. I find something therapeutic about the smell and feeling of freshly washed clothes and folding them for the week ahead. Even on the busiest days, the repetitive nature of folding feels like a mindful activity to me. **Part of the appeal of laundry for me is the instant results.** And a well-ordered, tidy laundry room and routine are part of that.

Did you know that wrinkles form on clothes as they cool? So by leaving your items in the dryer without removing them it actually creates more work with ironing later. Getting organised with laundry can seem like a daunting task at first, but as with any routine shift, it's all about mindset. **In this chapter I'll be sharing really simple and practical ways to get on top of your laundry and keep your laundry room a place that you can actually be proud of.**

CLEANING *playlist*

Clean in 15

One of the simplest ways to avoid laundry piling up in your home is to find a regular schedule. On one end of the spectrum, if you have a newborn or small baby, you may find yourself doing a few loads of laundry a day, but if you live alone or with a partner, it may be more like once or twice a week. Every household is different, but a simple rule of thumb is to run a load as soon as your laundry basket is full.

As mentioned above, using the delay start function on your washing machine is a great time-saving trick to make your 15-minute clean so much easier. Whether you do your Clean in 15 daily or weekly depends on your household and your lifestyle, so find the frequency that works best for you. Watch that washing pile stay under control!

CHECKLIST

- ☐ Put on a load of laundry
- ☐ Fold load of laundry
- ☐ Pack away laundry
- ☐ Clear lint from the dryer filter after each load
- ☐ Leave the door to the washing machine open after each load to avoid mould build-up
- ☐ Iron any clothes that you need during the week
- ☐ Place items for hand-washing in a separate bag

DAILY / WEEKLY LAUNDRY CLEAN

TIPS AND TRICKS TO *save time on laundry*

SORT IT OUT

Sorting laundry allows you to use different wash cycles and temperatures and helps make your clothes last longer. It prevents fabrics bleeding into each other, or different fabrics rubbing together during the spin cycle. The best way to sort is between lights and darks, and heavy and delicate fabrics. Also consider which items should be hand-washed, and keep them aside too.

MESH BAGS ARE YOUR BFF

Make sure you have a few mesh bags to wash delicate clothes within. This helps protect them from stretching in the wash cycle.

SAVE TIME WHEN SORTING SOCKS AND JOCKS

Buy a separate mesh bag for each household member and name them using labels. When each household member needs to put their socks in the wash, they place them directly into the bag. The full bag can then go into the wash, and can be placed in the dryer or hung on the washing line to dry. That person is then responsible for sorting and folding their own socks and underwear.

KEEP CLOTHES LOOKING *newer for longer*

Keep your clothes looking new with these easy tips:

◊ Fasten all buttons and zips on pants and jeans so they don't rub against other fabrics and ruin other clothes during the washing agitation or spin cycles.

◊ Turn clothes inside out before washing them to prevent stretching and wear-out.

◊ Always leave buttons on shirts open as they can stretch and pull.

- As a rule of thumb, wash whites in hot water to keep them white and colours in cold water to prevent fading. Read care instructions to check the best temperature for your items.

- Add ½ cup baking soda to your load – this whitens whites, boosts colour and removes odours. It's great for musty gym clothes, towels and linens.

- Add a few drops of eucalyptus oil into your baking soda for a great stain remover.

- To keep buttons from falling off clothes or getting loose, use clear nail polish on the threads to keep them from fraying.

Honey, I'VE SHRUNK THE WASHING

If you've ever left your clothing in the dryer for too long and it's shrunk or lost its shape, there's a simple trick to restore it to its original condition:

- Fill a bucket of warm water and submerge your garment in it.

- Add ½ cup hair conditioner.

- Allow the garment to soak for 15 minutes.

- Rinse under warm water, remove excess water and lay the item flat on a towel.

- Gently shape the garment back into its original shape and allow it to dry. The hair conditioner relaxes the fibres, which allows the garment to stretch back to its original shape.

TIPS TO MAKE IRONING EASIER

◊ Hang items on the side of your clothes horse to increase the amount of clothes it can fit and reduce wrinkles from forming.

◊ If you don't have time to iron clothes, shower steam is a natural de-creaser. Place your item on a hanger and hang it in your bathroom while you shower. The steam will help release wrinkles.

◊ Clothes wrinkle when they cool, so remove clothes from the dryer quickly and fold as soon as possible. This will save you time on ironing later on down the track.

◊ If you have a dryer, place clothes that require ironing in there with a wet face towel. The damp face towel creates steam which can help remove wrinkles.

◊ Use tap water! Plain tap water can help remove wrinkles on clothes. You can spray plain tap water on wrinkles, or use the DIY wrinkle remover spray on page 176.

◊ Use a tea towel over delicate clothes before ironing them. By placing the tea towel in between the iron and the garment, it protects the fabric while still allowing the heat through to iron it.

DIY Wrinkle Remover Spray

Not only is this spray amazing on bed linens, it also works fabulously to remove clothes wrinkles. Always make sure you patch-test on the fabric before use.

You'll need:

- 2 cups water
- 1 tbsp hair conditioner
- Spray bottle

How to:

- Mix water and hair conditioner in a spray bottle.
- Spray a light mist on your fabric, smooth it and leave for 5 minutes to remove wrinkles while you're getting ready.

WHAT TEMPERATURE SHOULD I WASH MY CLOTHES?

Hot water: To keep white clothes white and for underwear and socks. Hot water is great at removing dustmites, so washing bedding in the hottest water setting possible is perfect to keep your bedding fresh and clean. Hot water can make colours run, so try to avoid it on colours if possible.

Warm water: The best option for coloured clothes to remove dirt and bacteria. This also helps remove tough stains like oil, mud or grease.

Cold water: A great option for all types of clothing that also helps to save on electricity bills. It's not as effective at removing tough stains like grease and oil, but is still a great option for day-to-day washing. Cold water works on any fabric and prevents colours from bleeding. Black clothes should always be washed in a cold water cycle to prevent the colour from fading.

WHAT ARE THE DIFFERENT WASHING MACHINE SETTINGS?

Cotton: This setting is perfect for most bed linens and towels, as it has a harsher agitation and wash cycle.

Heavy Duty: Great for towels, jeans or any heavy soiled items due to its longer duration and heavier spin cycle.

Synthetics: For your day-to-day clothing like activewear, T-shirts and sports clothing. This cycle usually has a medium agitation.

Delicates: For delicate clothing like silks and delicate undergarments. This setting has a much lower spin cycle to avoid clothes stretching in the wash.

Quick Wash: For those items that need a quick refresh but are not heavily stained or soiled. It's a short cycle for day-to-day items, but generally not recommended to include anything delicate due its high agitation and fast spin cycle.

Rinse and Spin: This cycle does not use any detergent, just rinses the clothes in water and spins them dry.

HOW TO WHITEN WHITE CLOTHES

White clothes are an easy favourite, but they're one of the hardest colours to keep stain-free! This DIY is powerful at removing tough stains and whitening socks, school uniforms, T-shirts and linens. As always, patch-test before use, as every fabric is different.

You'll need:

- Warm water
- ⅓ cup 3% hydrogen peroxide
- 1 cup baking soda
- 1 tsp dishwashing liquid

How to:

- Cover garment in warm water.
- Add hydrogen peroxide to disinfect the garment and brighten any stains.
- Add baking soda to help brighten and deodorise.
- Add dishwashing liquid to remove grease and oil-based stains.
- Allow to soak for up to half an hour, then place in the washing machine as usual to remove stains.

THE MAGIC OF DENTURE TABLETS

Denture tablets are another great way to naturally whiten whites! Simply soak the garment in warm water and add 1–2 denture tablets, then allow to sit for 30 minutes before washing as usual.

Tip When making any DIYs with hydrogen peroxide, always store them in a dark-coloured bottle and away from sunlight to keep the hydrogen peroxide active.

A QUICK GUIDE TO HYDROGEN PEROXIDE

Hydrogen peroxide is a mixture of hydrogen and oxygen that works as a non-toxic disinfectant and brightener, with no fumes that can irritate the lungs or eyes. It's also an antifungal and antibacterial, which makes it excellent for cleaning. You can often find it in your local supermarket or pharmacy in diluted percentages of 3% or 5%. Hydrogen peroxide found in percentages higher than these are usually for hair bleaching or industrial use.

Storage note: Hydrogen peroxide breaks down in sunlight or heat, so it's best kept in a dark area in an amber or dark-coloured bottle.

Safety note: Never mix hydrogen peroxide with white vinegar, as this can create harmful gases.

HOW TO REMOVE UNDERARM DEODORANT STAINS FROM GARMENTS

There's a simple and quick way to remove those dreaded sweat stains from your favourite tops. Sweat contains a high level of salt and when this mixes with the aluminium present in many deodorants, this causes yellow staining in the underarm areas. When dealing with sweat stains, it's important to act quickly. If the stain sits for a long time, or if it's placed through the dryer, it can set the stain.

You'll need:
- 1 cup 3% hydrogen peroxide
- ½ cup dishwashing liquid
- 4 drops eucalyptus oil
- Dark / amber-coloured spray bottle

How to:
- Mix hydrogen peroxide and dishwashing liquid into spray bottle.
- Add eucalyptus oil.
- Spray on stains and leave for half an hour.
- Machine-wash as usual.

DIY Laundry Colour Booster

This DIY helps boost fragrance in the wash and prevent fading from repeated washing. The mix of peppermint and lavender smells lovely, but you can use an essential oil blend you love or leave them out if you prefer a fragrance-free option. The chloride in Epsom salts helps seal in colour and helps prevent clothes fading, while the baking soda helps brighten, soften and deodorise clothing.

You'll need:

- 2 cups Epsom salts
- 1 cup baking soda
- 20 drops essential oil (I like to use a mix of peppermint and lavender)
- Airtight jar

How to:

- Add all ingredients to an airtight jar and shake.
- Add ¼ cup to each wash to keep your laundry smelling better and feeling softer for longer.

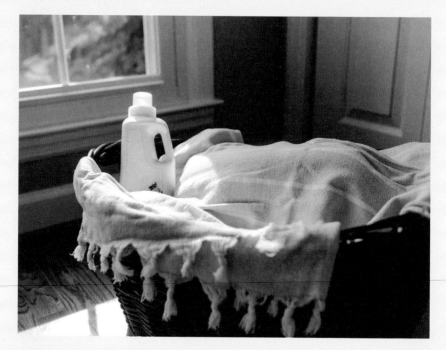

HOW TO REMOVE OIL STAINS FROM GARMENTS

These are some of the most dreaded stains. But I have great news – this DIY removes new and old oil stains on clothes, even the ones that have been through the wash before! The dishwashing liquid in this DIY helps draw up the stain from the fabric and the baking soda helps soak and remove it.

You'll need:

- Small plate
- 1 tbsp dishwashing liquid
- 1 tbsp baking soda
- Old toothbrush

How to:

- Lay garment flat on a table or benchtop and place the small plate under the fabric, behind the stain.
- Cover the stain with dishwashing liquid.
- Sprinkle baking soda over the stain.
- Use an old toothbrush to work this mixture into the fabric.
- Leave for 30 minutes.
- Remove the plate and wash as usual.

CLEAN IT *like you mean it*

Once you're in a more frequent laundry routine, you'll see that laundry pile stay under control – which is a big win! Every month, it's a great idea to give your laundry area a wipe down and declutter, as well as wash those less frequently washed items. This is all part of keeping the space hygienic for everyone.

CHECKLIST

☐ Declutter and clear unnecessary products from cupboards

☐ Drain the pump filter on your front-loader washing machine, if you have one

☐ Dust your laundry room shelves

☐ Wipe down laundry benchtops

☐ Vacuum and mop floor

☐ Clean laundry sink

☐ Deodorise tea towels

MONTHLY LAUNDRY CLEAN

HOW TO DRAIN YOUR WASHING MACHINE PUMP FILTER

If you have a front loader, the drain pump and filter should be emptied monthly to ensure the machine runs efficiently and to prolong the life of your machine. The drain pump filter also holds stagnant water, which can cause a lot of musty smells.

To drain the pump filter, simply do the following:

◊ Read your manual to find where your drain pump filter is located. In most machines, it's at the front bottom corner.

◊ Open the filter door and pull out the small tube, then pull off the tip of the tube and use a large bowl to catch the water that drains from the pump.

◊ Once all the water has drained, empty and clean the filter by hand-washing in warm, soapy water.

◊ Replace the filter and your machine is ready for use.

HOW TO CLEAN YOUR LAUNDRY ROOM

◊ **Declutter:** Remove any items that belong in other rooms. You can place those items into baskets and tackle them one at a time.

◊ **Organise laundry:** If you have piles of clean clothes, fold them into piles to go to each room, or place them in separate baskets for each household member to fold their own clothes.

◊ **Clear out cupboards:** Look for expired cleaning products, old sponges and cloths, or anything that isn't adding value to your laundry room, then do a solid cull.

- ◊ **Inventory:** While you're in your cabinets, also look at which items require restocking, and write a list.

- ◊ **Dusting:** Starting from the top, dust all areas of the room and wipe up any spills that you can see (like liquid detergent or cleaners).

- ◊ **Wipe down:** All countertops, cabinets and shelving.

HOW TO CLEAN YOUR LAUNDRY ROOM SINK

This is where clothes are soaked, cleaning rags are run through and stains are released, so it's important to clean regularly to remove those germs.

You'll need:
- ¼ cup baking soda
- 1 tbsp dishwashing liquid
- Microfibre cloth

How to:
- Sprinkle baking soda over sink.
- Add dishwashing liquid on top of your baking soda.
- Buff in with a damp microfibre cloth until clean, then rinse with water.

HOW TO DEODORISE TEA TOWELS

We use tea towels every single day, so they deserve some love and attention. If yours are smelling musty or have food and oil stains on them, there's a simple process that helps break down any grease build-up. The baking soda in this method also helps neutralise odours and soften the towels. This doesn't need to be done for every tea towel wash, but can be used monthly when they need stain removal or deodorising.

You'll need:

- Soaking bucket
- Hot water
- 1 cup white vinegar
- 1 tsp dishwashing liquid
- ¼ cup baking soda

How to:

- Fill a bucket with hot water, white vinegar and dishwashing liquid.
- Soak tea towels for 1 hour in the mix.
- Wash as usual on a hot cycle with usual detergent and the baking soda in the drum.
- Dry as usual.

YOUR GUIDE TO *cleaning shoes*

LEATHER SHOES

These can stain and scuff easily, so it's important to avoid scrubbing or using harsh cleaners that damage the leather. It's best to use a soft cloth and leather cleaner to remove tough stains. You can use a soft bristled toothbrush to remove tough scuffs gently. When cleaning leather, always finish with a leather conditioner to avoid the leather drying or cracking.

RUNNERS

These are made from different fabrics, so it's best to check the care instructions for your exact pair to avoid damaging them. Many runners can be spot-washed using micellar water, which is a type of oil-based makeup remover. Simply place about a teaspoon of micellar water onto a cotton ball or makeup pad and gently buff away the stains. It's powerful at removing scuffs and mud while being gentle on the shoes.

CANVAS SHOES

Keeping canvas shoes white and bright can be an ongoing task as they soak up mud and dirt very easily.

You'll need:

- Shallow bowl
- 1 tbsp dishwashing liquid
- ¼ cup baking soda
- 1 tbsp warm water
- Soft bristled brush

How to:

- In a shallow bowl, mix dishwashing liquid, baking soda and warm water to form a paste.
- Apply this paste onto your canvas shoes using soft bristled brush.
- Leave this paste for 30 minutes, then place the shoes in a mesh delicates laundry bag.
- Wash in the machine on a gentle cycle, then air-dry.

LACES

A simple way to give your shoes a refresh is by washing your laces. Simply remove from your shoes, place them into a mesh laundry bag then pop them into your next laundry load!

SUEDE SHOES

These often require a bit more TLC due to how delicate and difficult the material can be. For tough stains, you can try waiting for the stain to dry and then using a soft brush to brush away the loose dirt or mud. Many suedes can be washed using micellar water on a cotton ball to treat spot stains and help clean the surface.

DEEP *clean*

With regular cleaning of your laundry space, you'll be feeling so much more on top of the process that there shouldn't be too many items to deep-clean – yay!

If your clothes are starting to smell a little musty, it may be time to deep-clean your washing machine and dryer. Although it may seem strange that the items we use to clean can get dirty, the reality is that over time, laundry detergents can build up and create a film inside your machine in which mould and bacteria can build up.

Over time, this can create blockages that prevent your clothes from getting washed effectively, so giving your laundry appliances some TLC can help keep your clothes looking and smelling wonderful.

CHECKLIST

☐ Clean washing machine

☐ Clean dryer

☐ Deep-clean iron

LAUNDRY DEEP CLEAN

HOW TO CLEAN YOUR FRONT-LOADER WASHING MACHINE

Start by reading your washing machine's manual to see the best way to maintain your machine. If you don't have a copy of it, many manuals can be found online by typing in your washing machine's serial number.

You'll need:

- Bucket
- 1 tsp dishwashing liquid
- 5 cotton balls
- ¼ cup 3% hydrogen peroxide
- White vinegar or commercial washing machine cleaner (you can buy these at most supermarkets)

How to:

- Empty drain pump filter into a bucket. (You can check your manual to see where yours is located – it's usually at the front base of the machine. See the instructions about this in the section on page 183.)
- Remove filter and hand-wash with dishwashing liquid in the sink before returning it.
- Remove any parts you can detach, like the detergent tray, and wash them in the sink in warm water.
- Soak 5 cotton balls in 3% hydrogen peroxide and place the soaked balls in your washing machine's seal for 30 minutes to remove any mould.
- Remove cotton balls and wipe down the seal with hot water.
- Run the machine on the hottest setting empty with a cleaner of your choice, either vinegar or a commercial cleaner.

HOW TO CLEAN YOUR TOP-LOADER WASHING MACHINE

Top loaders also require occasional deep cleaning. It's a similar process to front loaders, with a few simple changes.

You'll need:

- 3 cups white vinegar or commercial cleaner
- DIY multipurpose spray

How to:

- Remove any parts you can detach, like the detergent tray, and hand-wash them in the sink in warm water.
- Turn on the washing machine to the hottest setting.
- Add white vinegar or commercial washing machine cleaner into the drum while the water is filling into the machine, to allow it to mix properly with the water.
- Allow the cycle to finish, then use the DIY multipurpose spray to clean the rim of the washing machine and any visible soap scum or build-up.

Opt for a natural laundry detergent that's kinder to the environment – one with plant-based ingredients and which is high-concentration – to avoid detergent build-up.

TIPS TO KEEP YOUR WASHING MACHINE CLEANER FOR LONGER

◊ Each time you finish a load of laundry, empty the clothes from the washing machine straight away to avoid musty odours.

◊ After each wash, pull out the detergent tray and allow it to air-dry to avoid bacteria and mould build-up.

◊ After each wash, leave the door of the washing machine wide open to air-dry. This will keep the machine smelling fresh.

◊ If you have a front-loader washing machine, wipe down the front rubber seal after each use to avoid stagnant water that causes mould.

HOW TO CLEAN YOUR DRYER

If your dryer is leaving your clothes smelling damp or musty, it could be time for a deep clean. As well as emptying the lint filter after every use, giving your dryer a deeper clean can help keep it functioning in top condition.

◊ Every few months, remove your dryer lint filter and wash it in warm, soapy water and let it dry completely before returning it.

◊ Use the narrow crevice attachment on your vacuum cleaner to remove the lint that's built up deeper in the crevices of your machine.

◊ Wipe down the exterior of the machine with the multipurpose spray and a microfibre cloth.

HOW TO DEEP-CLEAN YOUR IRON

If you find your iron is not gliding smoothly, if it's damaging your clothes or if it's sputtering water, it could be time for a clean. It's very quick and easy to get your iron working like new again.

You'll need:
- A microfibre cloth or old rag
- White vinegar

How to:
- Make sure your iron is cool, switched off and unplugged from the wall outlet.
- Soak a microfibre cloth or rag in white vinegar.
- Place your iron on the rag so it covers the plate.
- Wait for 30 minutes, then wipe with a clean cloth and warm water.

THE DREAM CLEAN

Organising

A well-organised laundry room can help you save time, maximise space and make the whole process simpler from start to finish. The laundry is a great space to utilise labels to be able to find small bits and pieces that are stored around the home, like allen keys for furniture or extra light bulbs. Here are my top tips for organising your laundry:

ONLY KEEP WHAT YOU USE

This is a common theme throughout each chapter, but it's perhaps most relevant here – the first step to a clean and organised laundry room is to only have the items you actually use in the room. It's time to declutter extraneous items and move them to their correct 'homes'. While you're doing this, make sure the items you keep in your laundry have a home too. This could be wire baskets for cleaning supplies, laundry supplies, extra light bulbs, tools or first aid kits.

KEEP IT ACCESSIBLE

Keep your detergents, cleaning products and frequently used items easy to reach. Using beautiful jars that match your laundry's interior for products like laundry powder, stain removers and softeners is a great way to mix functionality and style. Keep them on the benchtop to add to your laundry's décor.

SEPARATE WASHING BASKETS

If space allows, another time-saving trick is for each member of the family / household to have their own washing basket. This way everyone can do their own loads of laundry and be responsible for the washing and drying of their own clothes. This can be helpful if you have older children or a housemate.

Another option is to separate laundry baskets based on wash types, so a separate basket for whites, colours, heavy items and delicates.

When taking the clean clothes off the line, you can use the same baskets to categorise folded washing as well.

LET'S HANG OUT

Keep an area free for hanging space in your laundry. If you're low on space, this could be a retractable clothes line from the wall, or it could be a larger hanging rack. When clothes are hot out of the dryer, hang them straight onto hangers to prevent wrinkles from forming and save yourself ironing time later.

PET SUPPLIES STORAGE SOLUTIONS

Pets can entail a lot of storage items, like food, medicines, grooming items, dishes and vitamins. Your laundry is the perfect place to store these.

◊ Keep all items together in a specific cupboard or shelf, so you know exactly where to look for them.

◊ Customise storage sections or baskets in your cupboard or shelf for different items like:
   - Food, treats and bowls
   - Toys
   - Walking – leashes, collars, waste disposal
   - Grooming and medication

◊ Tuck a pet bed into an area of your laundry as a quiet place for your pet to rest, and include some of their favourite toys.

If pet fur gets all over your home and furniture and is difficult to clean, use a rubber glove to pick it up with ease. Simply place on a rubber glove and run it across your furniture to remove pet hair quickly and easily.

MAXIMISE STORAGE SPACE WITH SUITCASES

When suitcases are in storage, they can take up a lot of space. Depending on whether you travel frequently or infrequently, you can actually use your empty suitcases as extra storage space within your home. Fill empty suitcases with Christmas supplies, outgrown sentimental clothes or other items when not in use. When you're back from your holiday, place all the items back in before storing it away again.

TIPS TO PACK YOUR SUITCASE

◊ **Roll your clothes:** You've probably heard this one before, but rolling your clothes is a great way to reduce wrinkles and fit much more into your suitcase.

◊ **Use travel space bags:** These bags are great to organise your clothing, and you can use them as dirty clothes bags once you arrive at your destination. You can find some that are colour coded, or even ones that compress to allow for more clothes to fit in.

◊ **Use shoes as storage:** Don't forget the space inside your shoes, hats or any bulky items to fit in more storage space. Use shower caps on the bottom of your shoes to prevent your clothes getting dirty.

◊ **Use a straw:** Cut a small section of a straw and place your necklaces through it before fastening them to avoid them tangling. Use pill containers to store small jewellery, to avoid it going missing.

◊ **Use travel bottles:** Decant your large liquid items into smaller travel-sized bottles to avoid carrying unnecessary weight.

◊ **Wear your bulky items:** Avoid carrying heavy items by wearing them on the flight or journey over.

◊ **Pack smart:** Pack items that you can make a few different outfits with or are versatile and can be dressed up or down.

Styling

When it comes to styling the laundry, the key is to keep it simple. The laundry is a very practical and functional space in the home, so the priority is to keep it as clear and clean as possible.

THINK SINK: Create a small vignette near your sink area. This could be a small tray with a handwash, hand cream and small wooden scrubbing brush or soap. Add a candle around this area to keep your laundry smelling lovely and add a plant for a pop of greenery.

BENCHTOPS: I always think keeping benchtops clear and uncluttered is key to creating a neat and calm laundry space. If you prefer to have some items on your benchtops, you can opt to display things like a stack of freshly washed towels or storage baskets. Baskets are also a great way to bring in colour and texture.

HANGING SPACE: Incorporate some hanging space in your laundry with a retractable clothes line or standing clothes line. As mentioned above, this extra hanging space will make a lot of difference to cutting down on ironing and preventing clutter in your laundry.

WASHING BASKETS: These don't need to be boring! Choose a gorgeous option that suits your home décor scheme, or opt for one in your favourite colour to make laundry a bit more fun.

Laundry routines and checklists

CHECKLIST

DAILY / WEEKLY LAUNDRY CHECKLIST

- ☐ Put on a load of laundry
- ☐ Fold load of laundry
- ☐ Pack away laundry
- ☐ Clear lint from the dryer filter after each load
- ☐ Leave the door to the washing machine open after each load to avoid mould build-up
- ☐ Iron any clothes that you need during the week
- ☐ Place items for hand-washing in a separate bag

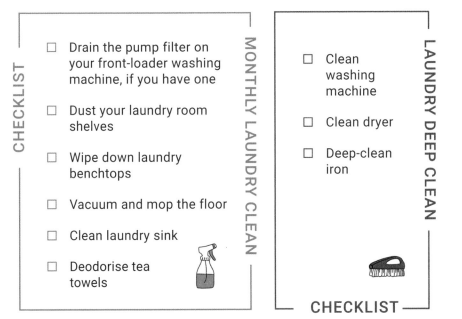

MONTHLY LAUNDRY CLEAN

CHECKLIST

- ☐ Drain the pump filter on your front-loader washing machine, if you have one
- ☐ Dust your laundry room shelves
- ☐ Wipe down laundry benchtops
- ☐ Vacuum and mop the floor
- ☐ Clean laundry sink
- ☐ Deodorise tea towels

LAUNDRY DEEP CLEAN

- ☐ Clean washing machine
- ☐ Clean dryer
- ☐ Deep-clean iron

CHECKLIST

CHAPTER 6

Outdoor
areas

In real estate, the terms 'kerb appeal' and 'street presence' describe the appeal of a home when you walk up to it for the first time. Things like how neatly the front garden is presented, the colour of the external paint of your home, whether there are cobwebs and if your windows are clean make a big difference to the street appeal of your home. These small details add up to the overall impression you give visitors – and yourself – when you arrive, so **an outdoor clean and refresh can be one of the simplest ways to make your home feel inviting.**

And don't forget the backyard, of course! This is where so many memories are made, from kids' birthday parties to alfresco barbecues, in the pool or on the deck. An inviting outdoor area helps you make the most of the warmer months by creating a space to host your family and friends.

Cleaning the exterior areas of your home doesn't have to be a daunting task. It's best to start with decluttering what you don't use. Many homes, especially if they've been lived in for a long time, have things like broken outdoor furniture, old light fittings, rusted bikes and old paint cans. These can often be donated or thrown away depending on their condition. If your council has a hard rubbish collection, this is a great time to look outside at the things you no longer use.

After that, it's a lot easier to stay on top of keeping these areas neat and tidy. Your use of outdoor spaces will depend on climate and geography, of course, so if you aren't outside too many months of the year, invest in some waterproof furniture covers, for example. **Small changes like this can make these spaces low-maintenance**, and in this chapter I'll show you how creating a well-styled outdoor area is easier than you think!

CLEANING *playlist*

Clean IN 15

The outdoor area often doesn't need daily maintenance. Unless you have deciduous trees or an area that requires more frequent sweeping, a 15-minute clean once a week is often enough to keep the area neat and tidy. Wiping down outdoor furniture once a week helps keep dust, dirt and excess water away and keeps your furniture looking fresh and clean. Staying on top of these small tasks allows you to entertain unexpected guests if they drop by!

CHECKLIST

- ☐ Wipe down outdoor furniture
- ☐ Sweep leaves from decking
- ☐ Store chair cushions out of the elements undercover
- ☐ Leaf-blow pathways
- ☐ Check outdoor light fittings and clean if dirty

WEEKLY OUTDOOR CLEAN

HOW TO CLEAN WOODEN OR WICKER OUTDOOR FURNITURE

You can revamp dull wood or wicker furniture with the right cleaning products. As wood is a porous material, it's important to take care of it to avoid tarnishing the furniture.

You'll need:
- Vacuum
- Spray bottle
- 1 cup warm water
- 1 tbsp castile soap
- Microfibre cloth or rag

How to:
- Vacuum your outdoor furniture to remove loose dirt and debris.
- In a spray bottle, mix warm water with castile soap.
- Spray this solution on your wooden furniture and clean with a microfibre cloth or rag to remove stains and dirt from your furniture.
- If any soap residue remains, make sure to wipe it down again with a slightly damp rag, then wipe the furniture dry.

HOW TO CLEAN IRON OUTDOOR FURNITURE

Regular cleaning is important for iron outdoor furniture as it is prone to oxidisation and rust from rain, and fading from direct sunlight. This simple method leaves it looking fresh and new.

You'll need:
- Vacuum
- Spray bottle
- 1 cup warm water
- 1 cup white vinegar
- Old toothbrush or scrub brush
- Microfibre cloth or rag

How to:
- Vacuum your outdoor furniture to remove loose dirt and debris.
- In a spray bottle, mix warm water with white vinegar.
- Spray on your iron furniture then clean the surface with a microfibre cloth or rag. Use an old toothbrush or scrub brush to get into any hard-to-reach areas.
- Wipe all surfaces clean with a damp rag.

DIY Outdoor Cushion Cleaner

With exposure to dust, rain, sand and pollen, outdoor furniture can get dirty very quickly and begin to look dull. Quickly wiping down your outdoor furniture every week – during the months you use it – can freshen its appearance. You can use this cleaner more frequently in the warmer months when you're entertaining or relaxing in your outdoor area. This DIY can also be used on any outdoor soft furnishing, including outdoor umbrellas or rugs. Note: Always patch-test this mix before use, as all fabrics are different.

You'll need:

- Vacuum
- Bowl
- 2 cups hot water
- ¼ cup 3% hydrogen peroxide
- 1 tbsp dishwashing liquid
- Rag or brush

How to:

- If your outdoor furniture is covered with leaves and dirt, vacuum the furniture and remove cobwebs.
- Mix the hot water, hydrogen peroxide and dishwashing liquid together in a bowl.
- Dip a rag or brush into the bowl and use this mix to spot-clean your outdoor cushions and remove spot stains, mould spots and mildew.

Tip In the colder months, you can buy furniture covers to help protect your furniture from the elements. Place these in the washing machine every 3–6 months to give them a deep clean. It's always best to try to leave outdoor furniture cushions indoors or undercover to avoid them gathering mould or fading in the rain.

TIPS AND TRICKS TO KEEP YOUR OUTDOOR FURNITURE *looking fresh*

◊ Close your outdoor umbrellas when not in use to avoid dirt, bird droppings and fading. Use the cover of your umbrella to keep it looking fresh while packed away.

◊ Wipe down your outdoor furniture frequently to avoid mould, rust and fading.

◊ Tilt your furniture during rain or storms so water slides off and doesn't pool on it.

◊ Store outdoor cushions undercover or indoors when raining to avoid stains forming on them.

◊ Keep the DIY outdoor cushion cleaner (see page 202) handy and in a storage area outdoors for quick access for stains and spills.

◊ Check your outdoor light fittings to see if there are any bugs or dirt in them. If so, simply remove the cover and wipe them to make the area cleaner and brighter.

Although you don't need to spend a lot of money to be able to maintain the outdoor area of your home, there are a few tools that you can opt to invest in that make the process quicker and easier!

PRESSURE WASHER

This uses jets of water at very high pressures concentrated on a small area to remove stuck-on dirt, soil and debris without scrubbing. Pressure washers can be used on bricks, outdoor tiles, porches, balustrades, roofs, gutters, concrete and kids' play equipment to clean the areas quickly. They're a great way to save time when cleaning, but they use a lot of water.

POWER SCRUBBER

I've mentioned before the benefits of a power scrubber for indoor cleaning, and those same benefits apply outside the home. With different heads, power scrubbers can be used to clean brickwork, the car, windows, decking and grout on outside tiles.

WATER REPELLENT

To avoid constant water marks and cleaning of windows and pool fences, investing in a water repellent may be a simple way to save you lots of time! Simply apply after you clean your windows. The repellent coats the glass so water beads off, instead of sitting on the glass and leaving marks.

CLEAN IT *like you mean it*

Every month it's good to give the outdoor areas a bit of a deeper clean. By cleaning items like decking and rails every month, you can stay on top of the task and avoid it from building up with dirt or cobwebs. That'll make the job easier and more manageable each time!

CHECKLIST

- ☐ Clean patio / deck
- ☐ Wipe balcony railings
- ☐ Clean barbecue
- ☐ Clean out car

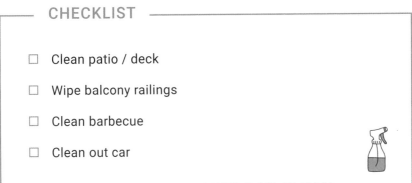

MONTHLY OUTDOOR CLEAN

HOW TO CLEAN YOUR OUTDOOR PATIO / DECK

Let's get one thing straight – it's impossible to keep your decking clean all year around, so don't be too hard on yourself! Dirt, dust, leaves and rain will collect within days of cleaning. But there are a few things you can do to maintain the look of your deck, and monthly TLC will leave it looking fresh and clean.

You'll need:

- Broom
- 1 tbsp dishwashing liquid
- Bucket of warm water

How to:

- Blow or sweep all leaves and debris away from your decking area.
- Mix dishwashing liquid into bucket of warm water. Use this soapy solution, or a decking cleaner of your choice, to clean your decking with the broom.
- Scrub the whole patio down with the mixture and a broom, then hose down the water to remove.

If you have a pressure cleaner, this is a great time-saving alternative to the above method to leave your decking sparkling clean.

HOW TO CLEAN A BARBECUE

This can be a really tricky area to clean, with lots of burnt-on grease and coal. For this reason, it's always best to wipe down after each use. But to get it ready for your next barbecue, you can follow these easy steps to get your backyard ready to entertain!

You'll need:
- Scraper
- A sink or bucket of warm water
- 2 tbsp dishwashing liquid
- ½ cup baking soda
- Scourer or power scrubber
- ½ cup white vinegar
- Spray bottle

How to:
- While the grill is still warm, use a scraper to remove any burnt parts.
- Turn off the barbecue and disconnect the gas.
- Once they've cooled, remove the hotplates.
- Fill up a sink or tub with warm water and add dishwashing liquid until it's soapy.
- Place your trays into the soapy water and sprinkle on baking soda to help break down the grease.
- Use your scourer to clean your trays and racks. You can also use a handheld power scrubber to make this job easier.
- Use a mix of 50/50 white vinegar and water to wipe the exterior of your barbecue.
- Dry and replace the trays.

Tip Spray trays with canola oil to protect against rust and the elements.

TIPS AND TRICKS WHEN *cleaning your car*

While you're giving your outdoor area a spruce-up, it's a great time to clear out your car too. As much as I try to keep my car neat, between school and kinder pick-ups and the never-ending rush of after-school sports, it often becomes a dumping ground for food wrappers, sports equipment, arts and crafts, and paperwork. Depending on your lifestyle, the frequency you need to clean your car will differ, but here are some simple tricks to make the job easier:

MAKE CAR HEADLIGHTS SPARKLE

Cut half a lemon and dip it in baking soda. Rub the lemon across your foggy headlights to cut through grime and leave them sparkling. The citric acid in the lemon mixed with the gentle abrasion of the baking soda cuts through grime.

KEEP WINDSCREENS CLEANER FOR LONGER

Mix 1 cup white vinegar with 1 tbsp dishwashing liquid in a spray bottle. Apply this on your windscreen and buff in with a squeegee. Wait 10 minutes before rinsing off this powerful mixture that cuts through windscreen grime. Finish with a water repellent to keep it cleaner for longer.

SLIME!

Kids love slime and it's actually very helpful to clean your car interiors too. Roll slime around your car interiors including your cupholders, air vents and dashboard to collect small particles and clean easily in small nooks and crannies. You can buy car-cleaning slime online too!

CUP HOLDERS

Clean spills in your cup holders by wrapping a microfibre cloth around a drink bottle, then placing inside the holder.

SQUEEZE INTO TIGHT CREVICES

The area next to your car seat can be a lost void for so many hair ties, cards and coins dropped down there. Use a thin grout brush to clean in this section of the car easily and dislodge any hard-to-reach items.

Deep *clean*

Because outdoor areas are used more in the summer months, spring is the perfect time to dust away those cobwebs and prepare for the entertaining period. Get your home entertaining-ready with a big, thorough clean!

CHECKLIST

- ☐ Declutter and clean garage
- ☐ Clean windows
- ☐ Clean flyscreens
- ☐ Clean door tracks
- ☐ Clean pool fencing
- ☐ Clean gutters
- ☐ Hose outdoor bins
- ☐ Wipe down letterbox
- ☐ Clean outdoor lighting
- ☐ Wipe water and gas meters

OUTDOOR DEEP CLEAN

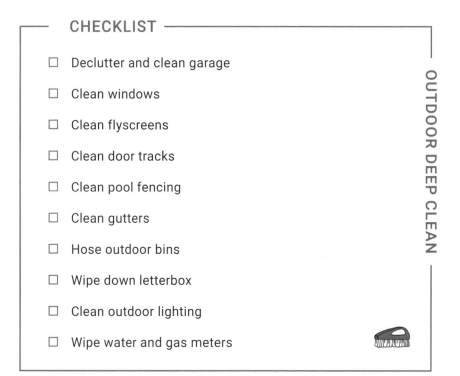

HOW TO CLEAN WINDOWS AND POOL FENCING

Doing this once a year is an inexpensive way to keep your whole home looking fresh and clean, increasing the 'kerb appeal' of your home. This DIY glass cleaner is powerful at cutting through dirt, bird droppings and grime to leave your windows sparkling.

You'll need:
- 4 cups water
- 2 cups cleaning vinegar
- ½ cup dishwashing liquid
- Bucket
- Squeegee

How to:
- Mix water, cleaning vinegar and dishwashing liquid in a bucket.
- Simply dip your squeegee into the bucket and apply this mixture to your windows.

HOW TO CLEAN FLYSCREENS

Dust and dirt can build up on these too – but we don't often give our flyscreens a clean to allow our windows to shine. Give them some love!

You'll need:
- Vacuum
- 4 cups warm water
- 1 tbsp dishwashing liquid
- Bucket
- Stiff scrubbing brush

How to:
- Vacuum the flyscreens to remove loose dirt and dust.
- Mix warm water and dishwashing liquid together in a bucket.
- Dip the scrubbing brush into the mixture and gently dislodge the dirt from the screen.
- Wipe the screen with warm water and allow to dry naturally.

HOW TO CLEAN RUST

Removing rust from the outdoor area can feel like a never-ending job. The quick and easy way to reduce the amount of rust on your items is by coating it with an oil-based lubricant, like WD40, regularly. If your items already have minor rust, this can be removed using lemon juice and baking soda. Cover the area with lemon juice, and sprinkle baking soda over the top. Wait for 20 minutes and scrub clean. This mix is powerful at removing minor rust spots on items.

Organising

Once your outdoor area is clean, it's time to organise it so that everything has its 'home'. Much of the outdoor area's storage space is within the garage or tool shed – these can often be large and undesirable areas of the home to clean, so a yearly clearout is important to remove all that clutter.

Choose a day for your garage clean when all household members are available to help. It's truly a case of 'many hands make light work'. Keep aside one entire day to complete the job from start to finish, and schedule it with your council pickup for rubbish, or an annual garage sale to make extra cash from items that you no longer use – after all, one person's trash is another person's treasure!

TIPS TO DECLUTTER AND ORGANISE YOUR *garage*

EMPTY: Start by emptying all shelving and cabinets, and place items in the middle of your garage floor. This will motivate you and your household to finish the task, as the garage can't be used until it's completed. (Sneaky, I know.)

Once everything is laid out in front of you, wipe down the shelving in your garage and group similar items together like:

◊ Sports equipment
◊ Christmas decorations
◊ Tools
◊ Paint cans
◊ Wires and cables
◊ Car cleaning supplies
◊ Pool cleaning supplies

DONATE: While you're laying out and categorising your items, look at which items you no longer use that can be donated or thrown away. Keep them in a separate area for donation or disposal.

CREATE ZONES: Once all items are sorted into categories, create zones for the items you're keeping. Think about sports gear, holiday decorations, cables and wires, gardening tools, paint and car equipment.

STORAGE BOXES: Opt for large storage boxes for items that require stacked storage and use labels so you can easily identify what's inside the boxes.

DON'T OVERLOOK YOUR WALL SPACE: Look at which items can be hung from the walls to save space, like bikes, tools, hoses, power tools, rakes and brooms. Peg boards are a great alternative for tool storage, to free floor and bench space and keep tools easily accessible. A magnetic bar on the wall of your garage also helps to store tools and gardening tools vertically.

OPEN SHELVING: If you have an old bookshelf lying around, think about putting it in your garage to maximise your open shelving space. Depending on the size of the shelves, you can store paint cans, toolboxes and gardening equipment.

Styling

HOW TO STYLE YOUR OUTDOOR ENTERTAINING AREA

Now that your outdoor area is clean and tidy, it's time to transform it into an oasis that you'll want to spend your summer nights entertaining in, or your autumn afternoons to relax and recharge. When styling your outdoor area, look at which items you already have around the home that you can bring out into the space before you go shopping for new furniture or décor pieces. This is a great way to create a consistent style around the home, and also helps save money.

CONSIDER LAYOUT

Think about how much furniture you can comfortably fit in the space. You don't want to have too little seating, but also you want to avoid the space looking crowded or cluttered. Also consider how you use the space and how you entertain. If you have a pool, you may want to orient your seating to face the pool area. If you love cooking, a big outdoor table may be an important investment. Consider how sunlight moves through your outdoor area. If you entertain in the afternoon, avoid placing furniture in areas that end up being in direct sunlight.

TAKE A SEAT
Seating is key when entertaining, and if you entertain large groups, plenty of seating options is important. This could be dining table seating, a corner lounge and 'breakout' areas like sun loungers or armchairs. If space is an issue, streamlined furniture like bench seats, modular corner seating or stools are great alternatives to save space. If you live in an apartment building or in a wind-prone area, consider furniture that won't move too much.

REST AND RELAX
As well as creating a great space for entertaining, consider spaces for you and your household to rest, relax and take in the great outdoors. Adding a hammock or large armchair may be just what your home needs to create a beautiful breakout area in which to read a book or drink your morning cup of coffee.

CHOOSING YOUR COLOUR SCHEME
The outdoor area is a great place to have some fun with colour and personality! Consider adding colour into the space with outdoor cushions, pot plants, stools, and table decor and accessories. A real estate trick to add value to your home without breaking the bank is to paint your fence. Painting your fence a dark colour, like black, makes your plants look greener and makes the garden area pop.

LIGHT IT UP!
A great way to add a great ambience to your outdoor area is to add moody lighting and string fairy lights. Solar-powered lighting is perfect for this. Add a heater to be able to use your outdoor area all year around!

Outdoor areas routines and checklists

CHECKLIST

- ☐ Wipe down outdoor furniture
- ☐ Sweep leaves from decking
- ☐ Store chair cushions out of the elements undercover
- ☐ Leaf-blow pathways
- ☐ Check outdoor light fittings and clean if dirty

CHECKLIST

- ☐ Clean patio / deck
- ☐ Wipe balcony railings
- ☐ Clean barbecue
- ☐ Clean out car

MONTHLY OUTDOOR CLEAN

CHECKLIST

- ☐ Declutter and clean garage
- ☐ Clean windows
- ☐ Clean flyscreens
- ☐ Clean door tracks
- ☐ Clean pool fencing

- ☐ Clean gutters
- ☐ Hose outdoor bins
- ☐ Wipe down letterbox
- ☐ Clean outdoor lighting
- ☐ Wipe water and gas meters

OUTDOOR DEEP CLEAN

CHAPTER 7

Hosting

Hosting can seem like a daunting prospect, but it doesn't need to be – it should be fun! Don't overthink it. Try to recall the best party you've been to – what made it feel so special and memorable? Often what people remember about a party isn't whether the food was perfectly cooked or the table settings perfectly done – they remember the feeling, the mood, the company, the lighting, smells, music. Hosting is all about creating an environment that your guests will love and that will allow you to create lifelong memories.

My most memorable event was an event my husband and I attended called Dîner en Blanc, a secret picnic in a pop-up public space. It's hosted worldwide but we attended the one in Melbourne. We were asked to dress in all white (including shoes and accessories), and the invitation instructed us to meet at a location where a bus picked us up and took us to a mystery location. What I remember most about the event was that there was an amazing mix of music, fun and laughs. Although I'm sure the food was amazing, I can't exactly remember what we ate! What made the night so much fun was the full sensory experience surrounding the event, and how it made us feel.

You can bring that same feeling into your home. Don't overdo the preparation of small details – start by thinking about the atmosphere you want to create, and let all the details flow from there. And make sure your priority is having fun! Whether you're hosting a few friends, a dinner party, large gathering, barbecue or kid's birthday, there are some small but effective things you can do to make it a memorable event.

10 PLACES TO CLEAN BEFORE *guests* ARRIVE

There are a few key areas you may want to freshen up before your guests arrive. Although your family and friends may not worry about how your home looks, it's always nice to put in the extra TLC to create a space they can be comfortable and relaxed in.

1. **Sweep outside your home:** As this is the first area your guests will see, make sure to quickly wipe down your front porch and walkways leading into your home. You can add some solar lights in this area to brighten up the space and create ambience.

2. **Wipe down front door and remove cobwebs:** Remove cobwebs from around your front door and give the area a quick wipe-down so that it's fresh and welcoming.

3. **Clean entryway:** Pack away the clutter and add a candle for a great first impression. Nose blindness is when we become accustomed to certain smells, so we often don't know what our own homes smell like. Adding a candle helps add a fragrant aroma.

4. **Wipe down furniture:** Think about where you'll be hosting your guests, and give that area a wipe-down. This could include vacuuming your couch or cleaning your dining room table and chairs.

5. **Clean bathrooms:** Keep it simple – focus on cleaning on the toilets and sinks, and switch out the towels and bathmats.

6. **Top up soap dispensers:** If you have refillable soap dispensers in your bathroom, make sure these are topped up. You can also add a hand cream to your bathroom to add to the experience.

7. **Vacuum the house:** This makes a big difference – all it takes is a quick once-over to reduce odours and make the home feel fresh.

8. **Wipe down kitchen counters:** Chances are that your guests will come into your kitchen, so give the benchtops a quick wipe to make the area look presentable.

9. **Take out the bins:** This is a quick and simple way to make your home smell fresher and reduce odours.

10. **Freshen the air:** Stovetop potpourri are an amazing way to freshen the air in your home and are a wonderful natural alternative to candles or air fresheners.

DIY Stovetop Potpourri

These are a great natural fragrance alternative. You can pop them on as you begin or end your cleaning routine, or just before guests arrive, to fill your entire home with fragrance and warmth. You can use your creativity and find items in your pantry to create your own fragrances too. Enjoy as the smell drifts throughout your home!

'CITRUS AND SPICE' SCENT:

You'll need:

- Small pot
- 4 cups water
- 4 sprigs rosemary
- 1 sliced lemon
- 2 tsp vanilla extract
- Black peppercorns

How to:

- Bring water to the boil on the stove.
- Add all ingredients and allow to simmer.
- Keep topping up with water as the water evaporates.

'AUTUMN EVENING' SCENT:

You'll need:

- Small pot
- 4 cups water
- 1 sliced orange (or peels)
- 6 whole cloves
- 2 tbsp cinnamon
  (or 1 cinnamon stick)
- 1 tsp vanilla extract

How to:

- Bring water to the boil on the stove.
- Add all ingredients and allow to simmer.
- Keep topping up with water as the water evaporates.

'COFFEE SHOP' SCENT:

You'll need:

- Small pot
- 2 cups water
- ¼ cup used coffee grounds
- 1 tsp vanilla extract

How to:

- Bring water to the boil on the stove.
- Add all ingredients and allow to simmer.
- Keep topping up with water as the water evaporates.

'CHRISTMAS CHEER' SCENT:

You'll need:

- Small pot
- 1 sliced orange
- ½ cup cranberries
- 2 sprigs rosemary
- 2 cinnamon sticks
- 1 tsp cloves

How to:

- Bring water to the boil on the stove.
- Add all ingredients and allow to simmer.
- Keep topping up with water as the water evaporates.

Tip For a stronger scent simply add more ingredients, and for a weaker scent add more water. Keep topping up with water as it evaporates. Never leave your stovetop unattended.

HOW TO SET PLACES AT A DINING TABLE

When setting up your table, there are some simple etiquette rules to follow when setting up the table for a dinner party or more formal soirée.

PLATES

◊ Dinner plates should be in the centre of the place setting.

◊ Side plates go to the left of the dinner plate.

◊ Soup bowls are placed on top of the dinner plate.

GLASSWARE

◊ This goes to the top right of the dinner plate.

◊ The water glass is placed first, followed by the red wine or white wine glass.

CUTLERY

◊ As a rule of thumb, cutlery should be placed on the table in order of each course, moving outwards to inwards.

◊ Forks are set to the left of the plate. If you have multiple courses, the smaller fork for entrées will be placed on the outside, followed by the larger fork closer to the plate.

◊ Knives go on the right with the sharp edge pointing towards the plate. If you have multiple courses, the smaller knife for entrées will go outside, followed by the larger knife closer to the plate.

◊ Soup spoons are kept to the right of the knives.

◊ Dessert spoons and forks are to be placed in the area above the plate. Spoons face the left and the fork faces the right.

TIPS AND TRICKS WHEN SETTING UP YOUR
dining table

A tablescape is the combined feel of your table setting and centrepieces. Although it may be tempting to go all out and make your tablescape extravagant, I like to keep it simple. By not overcrowding your dining table, you're able to create an environment where guests can see each other and converse – setting the scene for a great party!

CHOOSE A COLOUR PALETTE: Look around your home's existing colour scheme and create your palette accordingly. Bring in colours from your tablecloth or greenery, for example. This will differ depending on the type of party you're hosting, of course – a kid's birthday may look very different to a formal dinner party.

CENTREPIECES: Start by choosing one element as your focal point – this may be something simple like greenery from your garden scattered down the centre. Then bring in items in complementing colours, shades and textures, for example candles or other decorative items. Choose a mix of glossy, matte and wooden items in different heights and shapes to add variety.

PLACE SETTINGS: Placemats or charger plates are a great way to bring in colour and texture to your dining table setting. These are placed under your dinner plates to add some colour and interest to your table. Also consider using linen napkins instead of paper to add some different textures. There are some great ways you can fold and present your napkins to make your event special.

Placemats designate the individual place settings, but they also help with cleaning so that mess doesn't spill onto the table or tablecloth. Charger plates are large decorative plates that sit under dinner plates. They are used in the same way as placemats but also have the benefit of protecting the table from heat from the food, and are often used for more formal occasions.

TIPS AND TRICKS WHEN *hosting*

Don't forget the ice: Make sure you have plenty of it ready before guests arrive, for all those drinks and cocktails.

Cocktail or mocktail on arrival: A fun way to treat your guests!

Don't overlook lighting: Overhead lighting can make the area look stark and uninviting, so opt for dimmable lights or candles.

Play music: This is so important to set the mood. Start it soft so that your guests can speak and converse at the beginning and then you can turn it up as the party progresses if needed (if things get a bit more rowdy, for example!).

The power of scent: Having fresh flowers or using a scented candle or stovetop potpourri can add another layer of ambience to your party.

CHAPTER 8

Gifting

I started appreciating and practising gift-wrapping when I was in high school. I noticed that it helped to create a moment, a memory, of the gift exchange. Seeing your loved ones' faces light up is the true joy of gift-giving – and when you put a little bit of extra thought and love into the wrapping, it makes the moment even more meaningful. **There are a few easy and beautiful styles of wraps that take very little time – and money – but look so impressive.**

A great way to manage the cost of gift-giving is by making DIY gifts. You can make DIY bath bombs using household ingredients, you can place items for a stovetop potpourri into a jar and tie a bow on the top, or you can place the dry ingredients for cookies in a jar with the recipe on the front. **Use your talents to make something you're great at.** If you love painting or pottery, these are gifts that friends and family love. One of my favourite gifts is a painting my husband's grandmother painted and some towels that she hand-embroidered with our initials – simple but memorable.

Gifting can also create clutter in homes and add to overconsumption. **To avoid this, think about practical gifts that your loved ones will use.** Things like laundry products, books, meal delivery vouchers and perfumes are great choices. Another great option is to play a game like White Elephant, or Bad Santa, where all members bring one gift with a budget limit. Everyone draws a number to determine the order gifts are opened in, and you have the ability to 'steal' gifts from anyone who has opened their gifts before you. It's a lot of fun and another great way to spread joy and cheer.

No matter what you're celebrating, whether it be a kid's birthday, Christmas, wedding or friend gathering, the gift wraps in this section will provide you with plenty of inspiration to make your gift-giving that little bit more special.

CRISS-CROSS GIFT WRAP

This gift wrap has been so popular since I first shared it online a few years ago. It's such an easy way to add some extra fun to your gifts.

PAPER SIZE
Height: The paper needs to be able to wrap ⅔ of the way up your gift, and cover the top only.
Length: The paper needs to be 3 times the length of your gift.

How to:

- Fold the base of the wrapping ⅔ way up your gift.
- Push the sides inwards to create two triangles.
- Repeat on the other side. This process creates a small triangle at the front, and a larger one at the back.
- Fold one triangle across.
- Fold the opposite triangle across.
- Fold the second set of triangles on top of the first ones.
- Secure the base of the gift as usual.

HOW TO WRAP UNUSUALLY SHAPED GIFTS

This wrap is perfect for those awkwardly shaped gifts which are difficult to wrap. Instead of spending extra money on a gift bag, use the wrapping paper you already have to create a gorgeous gift bag of your own.

PAPER SIZE
Height: Paper should be 8 cm longer than the gift on both the top and bottom.
Length: The paper needs to be enough to wrap around the gift comfortably.

How to:

- Fold paper around the gift loosely and secure with tape.
- Remove the gift from the paper.
- Fold the base upwards around 8 cm.
- Create a diamond on the base. Fold base and top inwards and tape.
- Place present inside through the top hole and fold top and seal.
- Punch holes using a hole puncher and add ribbon to the top.

HOW TO WRAP A BONBON

> **PAPER SIZE**
> **Height:** The paper needs to be tall enough to cover the gift, with an extra 5 cm on each side.
> **Length:** The paper needs to be long enough to comfortably wrap around the gift.

How to:

- Measure paper to fit around gift and tape.
- Remove gift from the paper.
- Fold in half.
- Fold sides inwards and cut the corners.
- Open the wrapping and place gift inside.
- Tie ribbon around the sides to create a bonbon shape.

HOW TO WRAP A CIRCULAR GIFT

These can be so difficult, but there's an easy trick to wrap around round bases – all you need is a pair of scissors!

> **PAPER SIZE**
> **Height:** The paper needs to be long enough to cover half of the top and half of the bottom of the gift.
> **Length:** The paper needs to be wide enough to wrap around the circular gift, but not overlap.

How to:

- Place gift on the paper and cut 1 cm strips in the top and bottom areas around the gift.
- Wrap paper around the gift and tape to secure.
- Fold strips inwards on both sides.
- Finish with a bow.

Don't throw away your leftover wrapping paper scraps. There are two easy ways to make a gorgeous flourish on your next gift.

HOW TO MAKE A PAPER BOW

PAPER SIZE

Height: The scrap piece of paper should be approximately 4cm tall.
Length: The scrap piece of paper should be approximately 8cm long.
(Note: This method works with pieces of paper of all different sizes, so these dimensions are guides only.)

How to:

- Fold paper in half and cut into a fish-like shape.
- Cut a triangle out at the end.
- Make 2 slits on either side of the paper and place them together.
- Wrap a small piece of paper around the middle to create a gorgeous bow.

HOW TO MAKE A PAPER PINWHEEL

PAPER SIZE

The scrap piece of paper should be an even square, approximately 4 cm x 4 cm, depending on how large you'd like your pinwheel.

How to:

- Fold the square into triangles on either side.
- Cut 4 slits along the folded lines in towards the centre.
- Place double-sided sticky tape into the middle of the square.
- Bring the 4 corners inwards into a pinwheel shape.
- Place on your gifts for an extra touch.

HOW TO WRAP A SHIRT

A shirt that is wrapped as a shirt will put a smile on everyone's faces!

PAPER SIZE

This wrap doesn't require any special sizes, but cut the same amount of paper that you would usually wrap your gift in.

How to:

- Wrap around your gift and wrap the base of the gift as usual.
- Roll the top down twice.
- Cut slits towards the centre just under the roll.
- Bring the sides inwards into a collar shape.
- Add a paper or ribbon bow to the middle of the collar.

HOW TO WRAP A WINE BOTTLE

If you've forgotten to buy a gift bag, or if you'd like to add an extra personal touch to your gift, here's a simple way to create a gorgeous wrapping from paper.

PAPER SIZE
Height: The paper should be a triangle shape with the top of the triangle the height of the bottle.
Length: The length should be minimum 10 cm either side of the bottle.

How to:

- Place the bottle in the middle of the triangle.
- Wrap one side around the bottle and tape this side to the bottle.
- Fold the opposite side into a zigzag.
- Tape the zigzag section at the bottom only to create a fan shape.

ALTERNATIVES TO *gift wrapping*

Newspaper: This can look chic if done right, with a few extra creative touches, and it helps reduces wastage. For example, for a birthday, you can use the front page of the newspaper from the birthday of the recipient.

Kitchen towels: Both to wrap your gift and as part of your gift!

Kids' artwork: Lay out a large piece of paper and allow your kids' imaginations to run wild. Let it dry for personalised, one-of-a-kind gift wrapping.

Baskets: A great way to present your gifts to look like hampers, and they're reusable!

MY DREAM CLEAN *checklist*

- [ ]
- [ ]
- [ ]
- [ ]
- [ ]
- [ ]
- [ ]
- [ ]
- [ ]
- [ ]
- [ ]
- [ ]
- [ ]
- [ ]
- [ ]

MY DREAM CLEAN *checklist*

- [ ]
- [ ]
- [ ]
- [ ]
- [ ]
- [ ]
- [ ]
- [ ]
- [ ]
- [ ]
- [ ]
- [ ]
- [ ]
- [ ]
- [ ]

Acknowledgements

They say it takes a village to raise a child, and this book has truly been like my third baby. So much love and thought has gone into each page, and it would not be possible without the contributions from a number of incredible people.

I wouldn't have been able to write this book at all without the support of my husband Robbie. Thank you Rob for always believing in me, picking up the mental load when I was writing until 2 am, looking after the kiddos and bringing me endless cups of tea − all without me even asking.

I'd like to thank my editor, Tom, who was there supporting and cheering me on through every step of this book's creation − from our early brainstorm sessions to our many, many design meetings and right through to publication. Thank you Tom and the entire Pantera team for offering so much insight, guidance and new perspectives to the book. You have been my #dreamteam

Thank you to my parents, who, when I told them I wanted to be an author at 10 years old, always believed in me and never laughed at my crazy short story ideas. Thank you for raising us to be strong and kind, and instilling in us the belief that we can achieve anything we set our minds to.

And importantly, I'd like to thank you, my followers − without you, none of this would be possible. It's sometimes strange to use the word 'followers' as I consider you my friends, and our community is one of the most lovely and supportive communities I've ever been part of. So much of the contents of *The Dream Clean* are shaped from your questions and comments. I am so eternally grateful for your love and support. Thank you.

Photo Credits